'TIS BETTER TO TRAVEL . . .

'TIS BETTER ~ TO TRAVEL ~

The Story of A.T. Mays and the Tourist Revolution

JACK WEBSTER

MAINSTREAM
PUBLISHING

Copyright © Jack Webster. 1989

First published in Great Britain 1989 by
MAINSTREAM PUBLISHING COMPANY (EDINBURGH) LTD
7 Albany Street
Edinburgh EH1 3UG

ISBN 1 85158 205 3 (cloth)

British Library Cataloguing in Publication Data

Webster, Jack
  'Tis better to travel: the A. T. Mays story.
  1. Great Britain. Travel agencies. A. T. Mays, firm
  I. Title II. Moffat, James
  338.7'6191

  ISBN 1-85158-205-3

Typeset in 10/12pt Goudy by Blackpool Typesetting Services Ltd., Blackpool
Printed in Great Britain by Billing & Sons Limited

CONTENTS

CHAPTER ONE

Who is A.T. MAYS?

THE name of A.T. Mays has come to be regarded as the Scottish synonym for travel – and not without good reason. For this remarkable company, based in the small Ayrshire town of Saltcoats, is not only Scotland's largest travel agency but one of the Big Five in the competitive jungle of Britain's travel and tourist industry.

Along with Thomas Cook, Lunn Poly, Hogg Robinson and Pickford's, it holds its own at the top end of that growth industry which has broadened the horizons of a population which once regarded a foray from Glasgow to London as a major adventure. Whereas the working folk from the West of Scotland would once look forward to their annual fortnight "doon the watter" – to places like Saltcoats, no less – they now venture to the hot spots of Europe with an ease which would have dumbfounded their forefathers. For travel was once the preserve of the rich and leisured classes; but no longer. Men and women returning from the Second World War, having served in Europe, North Africa or even the Far East, had acquired a new perspective on an undiscovered globe.

When the ravages of that war had been repaired and new prosperity was breaking upon Britain in the late 1950s, A.T. Mays was already in existence to serve the growing appetite for travel, to speed the masses on their way to a fresh notion of what a holiday meant. Much as they treasured childhood memories of Fair

Fortnights in Rothesay, Millport, Arran or Dunoon, they knew that the sonorous "Song of the Clyde" was just as likely to be displaced by "Singing in the Rain" as the dominant theme-song of their precious two weeks away from the work-bench or kitchen sink.

By the time the Swinging Sixties had been ushered in, the mass of the Scottish people was searching for the sun, more and more aware that, in life's short journey, they were due a greater share of torso-tanning than was permitted by their geographical placing in the north-west corner of Europe. So a whole new industry was flourishing as plane-loads of happy-go-lucky Scots took soaring into the skies, en route to Majorca, as a starting-point of foreign adventure which would eventually broaden out to the point where no journey was impossible, from Benidorm to Barbados or Bangkok.

The chances are they were booking that holiday through a branch of A.T. Mays, a name which grew slowly into their consciousness from the 1960s through to the 1980s but which, for all its success, has perhaps failed in one respect – that of making itself properly understood within the context of its own Scottish community. It was no doubt enough that A.T. Mays was providing an efficient and helpful service to its customers and that the origins and development of the company seemed of lesser importance.

Yet the romantic story of how it ever came about is a compelling tale which deserves to be told. I suspect that a venture into market research in any Scottish high street would produce a majority opinion that the firm was founded by a man called A.T. Mays.

So who is this mysterious gent? Does he live anonymously in some secluded corner of Ayrshire, having succeeded in keeping himself out of the limelight all these years? The first revelation must be that no such man as A.T. Mays exists. In fact the initials stand for All Travel Mays. But if that should seem to de-humanise the story, the second revelation will more than make up for the disappointment.

If the name of A.T. Mays came about in an accidental manner, the firm does indeed owe its existence to one remarkable man, James Moffat, a self-effacing Scot whose achievements in business are in direct contrast to the ridiculously low profile he has managed to maintain over half a lifetime in the travel trade.

The story of A.T. Mays is, in fact, the story of Jim Moffat, a man who could have chosen to project himself with the prominence of a Thomas Cook but has been contented to remain in the background of an astonishing tale. In essence, it is the story of an unsettled bank clerk in Ayrshire, finding consolation in breeding budgies and deciding to quit the bank and open a pet shop, with an adjoining travel agency in his home town of Saltcoats. How that precarious beginning was to blossom into a major force in the travel business is one of the most intriguing chapters in Scottish business history.

Emerging from the shadows on the occasion of his seventieth birthday, but even then with reluctance, Jim Moffat can be seen as the highly acceptable face of capitalism, a man who started out with such an abundance of naivety that one wonders how he ever surmounted the initial hurdles. A thoroughly likeable human being, plain and unpretentious, he has led the family business with a fair hand, gaining shrewdness with the years of experience but turning it to the

Dockhead Street, Saltcoats.

11

Headquarters of A.T. MAYS at Nineyards Street, Saltcoats – a former bank which Jim knew well.

advantage of his customers and never losing sight of his dependence on a loyal and hard-working staff.

From a Scottish point of view, one of the sheer delights of Jim Moffat's story is the fact that, through all the pressures to move his headquarters to the city of Glasgow, if not to the metropolis of London, he has steadfastly refused to budge from the little seaside town of Saltcoats, where the business started.

Indeed, the head office remains within the old Royal Bank building which he used to visit daily from the National Bank, round the corner, for the purpose of note exchange. The two banks were later to merge. When large tour operators and other moguls of the travel industry have wished to meet the owner of this highly significant company, they have found it necessary to beat a path through those winding by-ways of Ayrshire to the proud little town of Saltcoats, a whimsical adventure mixing perplexity with delight as the man at the helm would turn the conversation just as easily to the breeding of budgies and the price of bird-seed as to the organisation of flights on Concorde or cruises on the QE2.

Through it all, Jim Moffat remains the archetypal Scot, a canny and modest man with the shrewdness of a Carnegie and the twinkle of a Will Fyffe. At the personal level, therefore, it is an account of one man's rise to the top of a highly competitive branch of business activity, an endeavour which has all the colour of an adventure tale. At another level, it symbolises the whole story of Scotland's holiday and travel habits in the post-war period, the departure from a long-standing tradition in favour of foreign travel, with sunshine very much at the root of the quest.

CHAPTER TWO

The Bride from Down Under

IN the second half of the 19th century, when clogs were fairly widely worn by industrial workers in the West of Scotland, the Moffat family of Glasgow ran a clog-making shop in the city's Saltmarket. James Harkness Moffat, who had two sons and four daughters, would regularly inveigle his family into excursions to Ecclefechan, where they would set about cutting the timber from which they would later shape that solid footwear more commonly associated with the people of Holland. At £1 a pair, the clogs were sold to institutions like the Cooperative and the city transport department, which distributed them to their employees.

From that shop in the Saltmarket the Moffats would make their way home to a flat in Kent Road, which was near Charing Cross, by the Mitchell Library. One of the sons, James Miller Moffat (father of the future travel agent) helped out in the family business but was expected to carve out a living of his own. So he became a lawyer's clerk and pursued that occupation as a teenager in the 1890s, managing to save enough for a visit to London to accompany a close friend who was going off to South Africa to serve in the Boer War. While in London, by a curious chance, he met an Australian girl called Pearl Louise Jacobs.

Pearl Jacobs was the daughter of a Queensland lawyer, Henry Jacobs, who had the good fortune to land a windfall from the Australian equivalent of the Irish

Father, mother and myself in 1924.

Sweepstake and decided to treat his wife and two daughters to the grand tour of Europe.

They had no sooner reached London than fate intervened. James Moffat had apparently gone to a West End theatre show one night when, during the interval, a fracas broke out and he went to the protection of the Australian visitors, who were having a rather unsavoury introduction to London's theatreland. In the aftermath of appreciation being expressed, the Scots lad and the Australian lass found love at first sight, so much so that she did not return to her homeland with the rest of the family. Instead, and not exactly with parental approval, she returned with her new beau to Glasgow which, in its industrial grime at the turn of the century, damp and melancholy, must have been a prospect to put the full flush of romance to the ultimate test. What's more, the bleakness of a Glasgow tenement hardly measured up to what she had been accustomed to. In addition, she was soon homesick.

All that, plus the appeal of the Australian sunshine, seemed to have triumphed when James and Pearl Moffat, now married, returned to the young lady's homeland, where James undertook odd jobs around Northam in Western Australia. Now it was his turn to pine for his native city, not least his beloved Rangers Football Club, and when the couple set sail for Britain in the early years of this century, it was for good this time. James was coming home to run his father's clog-making business in the Saltmarket and the couple were bringing with them their first-born child, Pearl, who was born in Australia in 1903. The Moffats believed in spacing out their offspring. The second child, Bessie, did not appear until 1911 and it took another eight years for the birth of James, the main subject of this book.

By then the so-called Great War had come and just gone – a war which formed the great divide between the old order of things and the new – and among the upheavals which came to change the face of business, there were cheap boots and shoes flooding into Britain from the continent, with pretty disastrous consequences for Glasgow's footwear industry. The Moffat business went into decline but, in any case, the old grandfather had died and left it to his four unmarried daughters. In an age when women had less protection and fewer prospects of making a livelihood, it perhaps seemed sensible that the boys should be left to fend for themselves.

By that time, James Moffat was into his forties but he and Pearl decided to leave Glasgow and move down the Ayrshire coast to Saltcoats, where they opened a fruit shop and cafe in the town's main street. It was not a lucrative living but the Moffats worked hard at their new enterprise, James fitting into his new role as a small-town businessman with some reluctance. Daughters Pearl and Bessie helped their parents in the shop and little James played his part in running messages when he was old enough. In their Countess Street cafe, the Moffats served a three-course lunch for sixpence (two-and-a-half pence today) and worked 16 hours a day for seven days a week through those spring and summer months when the crowds would flock down from Glasgow and give little Jim his first taste of what was meant by a holiday season.

However marginal their living may have seemed at times, James and Pearl Moffat did make enough from their efforts to afford a holiday during their close-season. And they did not confine themselves to visiting other Scottish or even British resorts. No doubt as a result of Pearl's Australian background and the couple's previous trans-world travels, they ventured abroad for their own holidays, a situation which must have marked them out for local curiosity at a time when foreign travel was a rarity.

J. H. Moffat – aged one year.

18

THE BRIDE FROM DOWN UNDER

Apart from those who had served in France during the First World War, a journey abroad was usually undertaken on a one-way ticket – people emigrating in the knowledge that they would probably never see the homeland again, or young men going off to be policemen in Hong Kong or Shanghai. Sometimes a schoolteacher would take advantage of her long summer holidays to improve her language in France, coming home with tales which would be of little interest in today's more travelled and sophisticated society.

But James and Pearl Moffat were forever in search of foreign parts, ranging from Paris to Oberammergau, in southern Germany, where they went for the famous Passion Play. The children were left at home, however, and Jim Moffat remembers being farmed out to an aunt in Kirkwall, Orkney, and an uncle at Crosshill in Ayrshire. There was much excitement when the parents returned from their travels, thus a psychologist seeking hidden explanations for what shapes our destinies might well come up with an interesting theory about the seeds which were sown in the mind of little Mister Moffat and eventually turned him into one of the biggest travel agents in Britain.

His father had many rivetting tales to tell. Recalling that earlier journey to Australia, he was able to paint a lurid picture of having seen a black man eaten by a shark in Durban Harbour! On the lighter side, his father went to see the great Josephine Baker at the Folie-Bergère in Paris, while his mother recovered from food poisoning, having learned an early lesson about eating lobster in a Parisian cafe.

Listening to his mother's recollections, it gradually dawned on little Jim Moffat that she was strangely without an Australian accent. It emerged that she had been brought up by an English governess, further proof of the difference in social background between the Moffats of Glasgow and the Jacobs of Queensland, Australia. Despite the wealthier beginnings, however, the cafe owner's wife in Saltcoats doesn't seem to have benefited from inheritance. Indeed, it seems that Pearl was rather disowned by her family, who did not approve of her departure from the European tour to be married and, sadly, she doesn't seem to have had much contact with her parents thereafter. Nor did she benefit from her famous Uncle Charlie in Papua New Guinea, a wealthy man who gave rise to silent hopes that one day he would leave them all some money. Instead, he was captured by the Japanese during the Second World War and was never heard of again. In his earlier days, he had visited the Moffats in Saltcoats but complained that he couldn't understand a word little Jim said.

19

'TIS BETTER TO TRAVEL

If the boy had baffled the colourful Uncle Charlie with his Scottish accent, however, he was nevertheless building up impressions of the people around him. He remembered his father as a good-looking, quiet, unambitious man, bothered with fallen arches in his feet but asking very little from life and supremely contented with his lot. His weaknesses were Rangers Football Club – and budgies. He failed to infect his son with the former passion but did encourage him at an early age to take an interest in the breeding of the budgerigar, that aviary bird which owed something of its background to the Aboriginal regions of his mother's homeland.

Pearl Moffat, on the other hand, was a more out-going personality, much more ambitious than her husband and with a strong desire to see at least one of her family achieving something out of the ordinary. The family home was in Ardrossan Road, Saltcoats, and as a child Jim Moffat went to the local primary school, moving on to Ardrossan Academy at 12 but showing a total ineptitude for academic study or the art of passing examinations. He gained consolation, however, in the new-found game of rugby and quickly learned that you are more likely to be hurt if you fail to enter into the spirit of the game, with all its rough-and-tumble. Some might regard that as a valuable apprenticeship for the holiday business which was later to be his career!

Like many another pair of hard-working parents, James and Pearl Moffat wanted the best for their son. Having known the hazards of running their own business, with all its insecurities, they longed to see young Jim established in the respectability of a profession. If he was not cut out for university then banking seemed the likeliest alternative. Yes, how marvellous it would be if he could pass the entrance examination for a bank. The lad himself was less than enthusiastic but in those days before the Second World War parental influence was much stronger than it is today. Youngsters succumbed to the wishes of parents with about as much regularity as they tended to rebel in a later generation.

His parents did not take account of the fact that you need a certain type of temperament and make-up to succeed in different careers and Jim Moffat knew in his heart of hearts that he was not cut out for banking. But a bank clerk he became, as much to the parental delight as to his own private misery. As a 17-year-old, he trundled along to his first day at work in the old National Bank, which was later to become the National Commercial and finally the Royal Bank of Scotland as we know it today.

The National Bank branch in Saltcoats was in Dockhead Street, the town's main thoroughfare, and part of Jim Moffat's routine was to pay those regular visits to the Royal Bank in Nineyards Street to exchange notes. Little did he know that, in playing one of her little games, fate was giving him an early taste of a building which would one day become the symbol of a phenomenal success.

Back at the National, he came under the influence of "the agent", as many a bank manager was known in those far-off days. In smaller centres, the manager was frequently engaged in another career altogether and merely ran the bank as an adjunct to his other life. In this case, Jim Kirkland of Saltcoats was a local lawyer and a good guide to young Moffat who was, nevertheless, most unhappy in his work. "I had been in the bank for two years when the Second World War broke out," he recalls, "and I remember marching up and down as a recruit on the parade ground thinking that, for all its exhaustion, this was painless compared to banking!"

There was, of course, a certain status in having entered the banking profession, albeit at a salary which was only £30 per year, and Jim Moffat was later to value the training and discipline which taught him to undertake counting and paper-work with accuracy. The pattern of his future life was already working out.

CHAPTER THREE

The Unhappy Banker

LIKE the assassination of President Kennedy, everyone who is old enough tends to remember what they were doing when they heard of the outbreak of the Second World War on Sunday, 3 September 1939. Jim Moffat remembers it like this: "I was working in our garden in Saltcoats with a friend of mine, Graham Taylor, when my father and mother insisted that we come in and listen to the broadcast in which the Prime Minister, Neville Chamberlain, announced that we had gone to war with Germany.

"I well remember my mother, somewhat to our embarrassment, insisting that we should stand to attention when they struck up the National Anthem. The thought was passing through my head that, whatever lay ahead for us, this was bound to bring some exciting changes in my life-style."

Almost immediately, Jim Moffat volunteered for the Royal Air Force, with the intention of being a pilot, an ambition which did not succeed at first. Instead, his early posting was as an accounts clerk, completing the family allowances for new recruits, a job not too far removed from his work as a bank clerk. The accounts system of the RAF had not been designed for the mass of personnel now assembled for the war against Hitler and soon it was crumbling in disarray. Having acquired the standards of banking, albeit with no great enthusiasm, Jim Moffat was appalled to witness a sergeant coming round once a week to collect the family allowance forms which had not yet been processed – and dumping them in the waste-paper basket. The sergeant was following a well-worn services belief that the airmen would re-apply soon enough when they found that no allowances had come through!

The ambition to fly had not disappeared and Jim undertook his initial training at Padgate, where most of the young RAF recruits had to report in the early days of the war. When he came to filling in the questionnaire, he was honest enough to admit, in the query about being prone to sickness, that he could be sick on a swing or a roundabout. Nevertheless they sent him back to Scotland, to Prestwick Airport in his native Ayrshire in fact, where he was subjected to an aerobatics flight in a Tiger Moth. It was the first time he had been in an aeroplane and he had almost decided it would be his last when the pilot looped the loop then took the plane into a frightening vertical spin towards the earth which was guaranteed to eliminate the timid. Jim Moffat swears he was so petrified that he was quite unable to be sick! So they accepted him for training as a bomber pilot in 1941 and posted him to South Africa, under the Empire Flying Training Scheme.

"After the black-out and food rationing in Britain," he recalls, "what a joy it was to arrive in Durban, even with memories of the man-eating shark! This seemed like a land flowing with milk and honey, its scenery so superb and with a climate to match. Its politics apart, South Africa probably remains the most idyllic place that I have seen in all my world travels."

Jim Moffat was nearing the end of his flying training course at the Transvaal provincial city of Vereeniging when he flirted rather too daringly with death. While practising the art of high-level bombing, he found his aircraft had developed engine failure and made a desperate attempt at a forced landing on the bombing-range. It was not his best performance and the fact that the aircraft ended up as a write-off emphasises how lucky he was to crawl out alive, rescued largely by the efforts of his co-pilot, Tom Ruddle.

Most of the young men who became officers in the RAF at that time had some kind of public school background and Saltcoats Public School, in its Scottish connotation, did not fit him into that category. Nor did crashing an expensive plane exactly put him high on the commanding officer's popularity list. Nevertheless, he returned to Britain from South Africa in June 1943 and attended Central Flying School, where he became an instructor. It was good experience in piloting an aeroplane but not the best substitute for operational flying during a world war.

Wedding in Glasgow – 2 May 1944.

Wartime photograph: in the Air Force.

THE UNHAPPY BANKER

From schooldays before that war, Jim Moffat had been keeping the company of a butcher's daughter from Ardrossan, Margaret Robertson (commonly known as Margie, with a soft 'g'), a liaison which was maintained after he joined the RAF. They had met at a former pupils' dance in 1939, not long before he left for the war. The knife-edge of danger upon which everyone lived in that extraordinary period at least had the advantage of sharpening human awareness and the uncertainty of ever seeing each other again hastened many a wartime wedding.

With the build-up towards D-Day, all leave for the Army and Navy was cancelled and the RAF was likely to follow suit. So Jim came home on leave in early May 1944 and had the blessing of Bob and Meg Robertson to marry their 21 year-old daughter. Wartime weddings were often fitted into the bizarre circumstances of the time and Flight-Sergeant Jim Moffat had to make a somewhat unconventional dash from his base near Shrewsbury to keep that appointment with Margie. A friend gave him and his bicycle a lift in a light aircraft to a landing strip near Crewe. From there, Jim jumped on the bike and pedalled for all he was worth to the busy railway junction, catching a train for the north but missing his connection at Carlisle.

However, as in "My Fair Lady", he made it to the church in time; well, not exactly to the church but to the famous old Grosvenor Restaurant in Gordon Street, Glasgow, just opposite Central Station, which had the convenience of an in-built chapel and was the scene of many a Glasgow wedding. There, on 2 May 1944, Margie Robertson was waiting as a radiant young bride, in a borrowed white dress, with her cousin, Jenny Robertson from Kilwinning, by her side as bridesmaid. Flight-Lieutenant Alex Smith, a friend of the groom since school and rugby days, was best man. The couple sailed across from Gourock to Dunoon for a honeymoon at the Amet Bhan Hotel, where their purpose was soon revealed to fellow guests by a wedding picture in the old *Bulletin* newspaper.

Just as Margie's romance had blossomed in the Second World War, that of her parents had run a similar course in the First World War. Her father, one of the 13 children of a coal-miner from Kilwinning, was posted with the Ayrshire Yeomanry to Dunbar when Meg Neish from Edinburgh happened to go there on holiday. Like their daughter at a later stage, they kept in touch when Bob was posted overseas and they were married on his safe return, setting up home in Ardrossan, where they opened a butcher's business.

After school, Margie Robertson had gone to work in the office of a small manufacturing company before moving to the local explosives factory of ICI.

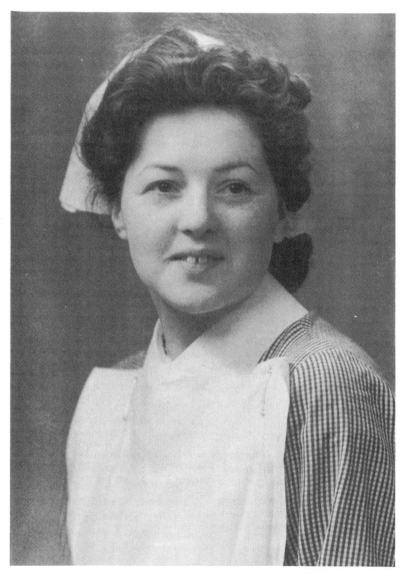

Mrs M. W. Moffat, as a nurse – aged 19 – in 1942.

When she was due for call-up to the Forces, she opted for nursing and went to the Western Infirmary in Glasgow. While working at the explosives factory, she knew that flying over there was forbidden to our own aircraft. So there was obviously something amiss on the day a plane came diving low across the Ardeer site. Looking out, she spotted the swastika of a German plane which had ICI in its sights. It was a frightening moment but, fortunately, no harm befell them.

Soon after they were married, the young pilot gained his commission and Margie went south to join him. They were just settling into a pleasant life on an isolated Shropshire farm when Jim was posted to India, as a flying instructor with the Indian Air Force.

Of all the young Indians who were trained to fly by Jim Moffat, he always remembered a pupil called Bandahar, an extremely promising young man whose name he would mention to Margie long after the war was over. "I often wondered how young Bandahar made out in life," he remembers. "The thought occurred to me again some 25 years later when I was visiting India in my role of travel agent. It was 1970 and I was flying as a passenger from Goa to Bombay, on an Indian Airlines domestic flight, when we were welcomed aboard by a Captain Bandahar. I called a stewardess and asked her if Bandahar was a common name in India. She thought it was very uncommon so I said, 'Tell the Captain you have a passenger on board by the name of Moffat. If that name means anything to him, I'll be happy to come up to the flight-deck to say hello.' She returned quickly to say the captain would like to meet me. So I made my way to the flight-deck and, as the captain turned his head, there was no doubt at all that here was my pupil from Jodhpur in the days of the Second World War. He greeted me very emotionally and once he had landed that Boeing in the darkness of Bombay, he turned round proudly and said, 'What do you think of that, sir?' Then he rather flattered me by addressing his crew and telling them that 'This is the guy who made it all possible for me.' It was one of those rich moments in life and left me with the satisfaction of knowing that, if I had done nothing else in the Second World War, I had at least trained one very good airline pilot of the future."

Among the memories which came flooding back was the fact that, having served with the Royal Indian Air Force, the young Jim Moffat could say he had seen some of the last remnants of the British Raj in that sub-continent. Having been stationed in the old Indian military town of Ambala, things that stuck in his mind included visits to the camp cinema where the three entrances made it plain that they were, respectively, for "Officers and their Ladies", "NCOs and their Wives" and "Other ranks and their Women". With all sorts of retinue around them, officers in the Indian Air Force were allowed to claim five-and-a-half times first-class fare when they were moving around the country. Jim saw a lot of India this way and benefited greatly from the ruling.

Back home in Britain, they had by now celebrated VE-Day in May 1945 and were about to mark the final ending of the Second World War with VJ-Day (Victory over Japan) when Jim received word in India that Margie had given birth to their first child, Margaret, an event celebrated in the officers' mess, where Jim Moffat was foolhardy enough to tell the bar steward that it was drinks all round. In the headiness of the occasion, the proud father forgot to cancel the order and the mess-bill which arrived at the end of the month was enough to drain all colour from the cheeks of a canny Scot. There was ample time to contemplate his folly on the troopship home from Bombay to Liverpool, back to demobilisation – and to see his new daughter who was already several months old.

After the six-year adventure of the Second World War there was no time to waste in resuming a civilian career, if only to support the wife and child who were now his family responsibility. In no time at all, Jim Moffat was back at the bank in Saltcoats, the same branch of the National where he had started in 1937. Nothing much had changed. Mr Kirkland the lawyer was still the "agent", offering a warm welcome back to the counter and a salary which had multiplied several times from those pre-war days but was still only £215 per annum. Jim's sister Bessie was moving from Sharphill Road, Saltcoats, so he bought her house for £800. If that figure raises envy among young house-buyers of today, it needs to be related to income and, at just under four times salary, it works out almost exactly similar to the present-day position.

So Jim and Margie Moffat settled into proper married life for the first time, Jim making the most of his daughter's infancy, having missed out on her beginnings. The youth of pre-war days, now matured through a war, had to bury some of his discontent with banking and try to make a success of it, as a means of livelihood. As it happened, he passed his examinations with honours but still harboured nagging doubts about his suitability for a banking career, a feeling that his face didn't quite fit for promotion. He had noticed that the brightest prospects were generally seconded into the Inspectors' Department.

If he entertained some notion of becoming self-employed, however, he had to remind himself quickly that he had no money and no particular idea with which he could launch himself. His parents remained proud of his banking status and his career was beginning to move in an upward direction, with promotion to the teller's job at Dalry and then as acting accountant at the Largs branch.

But still his heart was not in the job. Meanwhile, Pearl Moffat became ill in 1950. Among her reflective comments were that she would have liked to have had a large family and to see one of them turning out to be good at something. It had been her recurring theme and son Jim had longed to fulfil her dream but knew it would not be in banking. Pearl died in 1950 and was followed in that same year by her husband, James senior, both aged 69. They are both buried at Craigton Cemetery, Glasgow, a place which became so vandalised that Jim Moffat was appalled to find he could scarcely trace their grave. Their family home at Seafield Drive, Ardrossan, became the new home of Jim and Margie – and the double sadness of losing his parents did not exactly ease Jim's discontent. His constant moans about working in a bank were not helping to smooth an unsettled period in his marriage and the matter reached a head when Margie gave him an ultimatum. "Either give up the bank or give up me!" was the essence of what she was saying. That was it. Next day he went into the National Bank and handed in his resignation. He knew his parents would have been appalled at the surrender of all that security and pension rights which they so valued but the die had been cast and a speedy decision had to be taken on how to make a living.

Jim Moffat had never lost his fascination for budgies. That early introduction to the birds had made a lasting impression and the involvement became deeper when he came home from the war and his father handed over his entire aviary. This was something he knew about. So was there a living to be made out of breeding budgies? Perhaps not but it was also true that there was no such thing as a pet shop in the Saltcoats area. He could start one.

Another thought had occurred to him during his latter days in banking. More and more people were coming in to draw out money for their summer holidays. Where were they going? Well, their first step would be to Thomas Cook's or Llewelyn Davies in Glasgow, to book their way to the sunshine. Just as there was no pet shop in the district nor was there a travel agent. Not a single one in the whole of North Ayrshire. Immediate decisions had to be taken. So Jim Moffat would open a pet-shop in Saltcoats, as a main means of earning a living for his family, and his wife would run another shop where people could book their holidays.

31

The site of the original hut, where A.T. MAYS began in Manse Street, Saltcoats.

As an employee, he had never been a man of any capital but, during his time as a bank clerk, Jim had taken a passing interest in the Stock Market, reading his *Glasgow Herald* and *Investors' Chronicle* to see how prices were doing. With very little money to spare, he had begun to make modest investments in shares and the gods were on his side when he chanced upon the company called Regent Oil. The value of their shares began to soar when they were pursued and then

Jamie Moffat at Pet Shop opening aged six years.

bought over by the Burmah Oil Company. Jim Moffat's investment returned to his hand the first real money he had ever seen. It was £1,500 – and that was the starting capital for his foray into business. "So much so," he remembers with relish, "that we considered calling out new company Regent Travel!"

The pets came first, however, and in his original premises in Chapelwell Street, he opened a shop in November 1955, under the heading of ALL PETS. There is little doubt that enthusiasm and gusto outweighted forward planning because, far from being a shop for all pets, his opening stock amounted to a case of Kit-e-Kat and one of Winalot, spread thinly across the shelves.

On that very first morning he waited and waited to greet his first customer. At 11.30 a.m. – at last, at last – the first person crossed the threshold. Jim Moffat stepped forward for his historic moment.

"Can I help you, sir?"

"Aye, can ye mend ma fairy-lights?" asked the man.

"Fairy lights? But this is a pet shop," said Jim Moffat impatiently.

Oh. The man didn't know. Until last week it has been an electrician's!

Customer number two appeared at 12.30 with a seagull covered in oil. No, Jim Moffat couldn't do much about that either and the man left mumbling his displeasure.

By 1 p.m. he was making his way home for lunch to report that, in his first morning as a business man, he had not taken a single penny into the till. Over his meal, he began to wonder quite seriously if the bank might consider re-instating him! Well, business could only improve; and it did. He increased his stock and was on his way to establishing a modest success as a pet shop.

Within a few months, the Moffats were able to implement the second part of their business venture. On a nearby site, on the corner of Manse Street, by the bus-stop, they acquired a wooden hut which had previously been an undertaker's place, not the best of omens perhaps but lending a whimsical note to those early, faltering steps. Out of the ashes perhaps . . . Margie would look after the shop, which would follow the format of ALL PETS and be known as ALL TRAVEL. It was a simple concept but then most things connected with the Moffat business enterprise at that time had a fair coating of simplicity about them.

"We were dreadfully naive," Jim was to recall, with contained amusement. "Having no experience of the travel trade, we thought all you needed to do was put up a sign saying 'travel agent' and people would come in and buy tickets. It took us a year to discover, for example, that there was actually a travel trade paper

34

which contained about 50 per cent of the essential information we would need to run any kind of travel business."

As recently as the mid-1950s, foreign travel was still in a surprising state of infancy. Jim Moffat remembers his utter astonishment when Mr Kirkland, his boss at the National Bank, announced that he was flying down to London and back in one day. The journey would take three hours each way. Such speed of communication!

Matters like the need to become an appointed agent had been totally overlooked and it took several years before they were in a position to compete on an equal basis. But Jim and Margie did have one stroke of luck. Not long after they started, in March 1956, there was a huge increase in emigration from Scotland, with assisted passages available under the "Air Bridge to Canada" scheme. You did not have to be an appointed agent to sell tickets for that. The Moffats' ALL TRAVEL shop was now doing big business, though Jim remembers that, as people departed amid floods of emotion, he himself became caught up in family situations, with a regular lump in his throat. Many departed by sea from Greenock, waved off by parents and other relatives who wondered if they would ever see their loved ones again, especially the grandchildren. Such fears no longer obtain. The Moffats have survived to see emigrants on their way to foreign parts, in the knowledge that they may well be back for a long weekend within a short time.

Margie Moffat recalls those early days like this: "After a few setbacks, our agency opened for business that March day of 1956, with only myself and a delightful school-leaver called Minnie Kerr, who became our first employee. We set up shop in that little wooden hut, with railway tickets and a small selection of brochures, and happily wrote down the requests of our clients. When they went out at the door, we then tried to find out how we could make the booking! This system would certainly not be tolerated today but we were all innocents in the holiday market then – and had to learn very quickly. Soon we were employing a little blonde girl called Margaret Teevan as our typist and felt we were beginning to climb the ladder. We spent two happy years in that wooden hut, washing the windows and floors in our spare time and finding that we enjoyed the satisfaction of being able to provide the people with the pleasures of a holiday or simplifying the complexities of a business trip."

With the travel side thus taking root, Jim Moffat managed to secure a bank loan of £3,500 with which he bought an old manse in Hamilton Street, converting it into a double shop, so that ALL PETS and ALL TRAVEL could operate side by side, enabling him to flit through from one to the other without that diagonal crossing from Chapelwell Street to Manse Street. There was also room for some office space upstairs. Jim was now spending more and more time in the travel shop, leaving the pets to a female staff, though still plying between the two and being available when necessary. There was still a faint hint of comic opera about the operation.

The ladies in the pet shop had an unexpected visitor one day – a rat of immense proportions which was not on the livestock list at ALL PETS but had found its way through a store at the back. As Jim Moffat was summoned to the rescue of his petrified assistants, he came face to face with this snarling rodent, which suddenly came on the attack and bit his leg. A terrified Jim leaped into the air but fortunately landed plumb on top of the raging rat and brought it to a timely end, walking calmly away with the swagger of a John Wayne, under the admiring gaze of his lady assistants who thought he had been a hero!

With the top brass of the travel trade obliged to find their way to Saltcoats (where was that?) if they wanted to woo the boss of ALL TRAVEL, they could never be sure if they would find him there or at ALL PETS next door. A very senior official of the P. & O. Shipping Company arrived one day, a frightfully pucka gent in bowler hat and umbrella and apparently married to a cousin of the Queen, not that that mattered to Jim Moffat. On this occasion, the boss had to be summoned from the pet-shop, interrupted from his task of shifting large quantities of budgie seed. Dirty and perspiring as he emerged from his messy job, he felt obliged to excuse himself with an explanation that he had been labouring next door. Clearly taken aback by the eccentricity of the twin operation, the P. & O. gent merely pulled himself together and said, "How quaint!" Jim Moffat appreciated the humour of the situation.

The dual operation continued for the first few years, with Jim breeding and selling his beloved budgies, importing tortoises, extending his shelf stock from Kit-e-Kat and Winalot to merchandise like goldfish bowls – and clipping budgie toenails at a shilling a time: From such humble origins are business empires built.

All the while, Margie Moffat was coming to grips with the intricacies of travel, helped at first by Minnie Kerr only. As a challenge to the two ladies, Jim told them one day: "The first week you sell a hundred day-rail tickets to Glasgow I'll take you out to dinner." Not for a minute did he think it was possible. But soon they were holding him to his promise and Jim gladly obliged. In that first year, ALL TRAVEL pulled in £30,000 worth of business, not a volume that would leave

36

much in the way of profit but a reasonable start, especially for a couple who had launched themselves with such little preparation and research into the complexities of travel arrangement. At that stage, however, it was still such a struggle that they went home at nights and wondered if they were going to survive. But gradually, ALL TRAVEL established itself and they began to see daylight. Indeed, it became clear that the prospects there were greater than in the pet shop next door, not that that had been a failure by any means.

By 1958, Jim Moffat was giving his full-time attention to ALL TRAVEL and leaving ALL PETS to the care of a manager, George Hammersley, who took such an interest in it that it became his life's work in the fullest sense. In 1987, Mr Hammersley led a buy-out of the business, along with his son. By then, ALL PETS had extended not only to five shops, stretching from Saltcoats to Falkirk, but to a wholesale pet business as well, which is still thriving today.

First main-street shop in Saltcoats, 1958.

CHAPTER FOUR

What's in a Name?

IN 1959, there was still just the one ALL TRAVEL shop, situated in the heart of Saltcoats, but it was then that the Moffats took their first meaningful step towards being anything more than a single small-town business in a fairly off-beat corner of Scotland.

To gain the full flavour of the story, it is necessary to reach back to the early part of the century to find the origins of that elusive name "Mays" which was to dominate the business life of Jim and Margie Moffat. It all began in the Kingdom of Fife, in the town of Kirkcaldy, where a certain Dr McGlashan had a passion for geography and travel. In his medical practice he also had a patient by the name of Mays and together they went into the travel business, using the patient's name rather than the doctor's and opening at the town's Rialto cinema kiosk in 1928. Hereabouts the story takes a mysterious turn, with the reported disappearance of Mr Mays. But the business continued under the direction of Dr McGlashan's son Roland and was known as Mays (Shipping and Travel) Ltd, with a few branches around Scotland.

Eventually, after a long-established record, Roland McGlashan decided he wanted to sell the Kilmarnock branch of his business but, according to the ethics of the day, didn't want his family branch going to any Tom, Dick or Harry. But Jim was all right. He had been a banker and seemed a reliable and upright kind

39

of man who would look after it. So, at a single stroke, Jim Moffat's ALL TRAVEL enterprise moved from its apprenticeship stage into full professionalism, with all the valuable, licensed status that a firm like Mays could bring.

He now owned a well-known name in Bank Street, Kilmarnock, and thought it wise to capitalise on its familiarity. Some sort of combination would be best. How about calling it ALL TRAVEL MAYS, linking his own original idea to the better known name? That was what he tried to do but the registrar refused to accept it. Whatever the objection, the same registrar was prepared to accept the initials of ALL TRAVEL. So it was shortened to A.T. Mays and that is how it stands today, more than 30 years later. Jim Moffat was not wholly satisfied with the name at first and made several attempts to change it, not that he had any ambitions to substitute it with his own name. In the end he came to accept that it was short and rolled easily off the tongue and had already been accepted by the public as being synonymous with travel. So A.T. Mays remained – that elusive gent who had been elusive enough when he vanished from Kirkcaldy all those years ago. Now he was merely a fiction, an alias for a much more remarkable man who had gone from being a budgie-breeding bank clerk to a travel agent who would yet take his place in the upper echelons. But that was not the end of the connection with Mays (Shipping and Travel) Ltd. Just how Jim Moffat turned that story to full circle has yet to be revealed.

With the acquisition of that Mays branch in Kilmarnock and the establishment of a new company name, Jim Moffat had taken his first tentative step towards expansion. It was nothing dramatic and gave no hint of the possible extent of his future but it did give him the sense of having a formula for expansion, if that was to be the way of things. The pattern of the first 25 years, which would take him to the 1980s, is worth a study, not least by those who want to understand the mind of a highly successful businessman who has never claimed intellectual powers but whose plain, commonsense approach to life is an encouragement to us all.

Jim Moffat's expansion from that humble start in Saltcoats was subsequently financed from the profits which accrued. Whenever there was enough spare cash to buy or start another business, he did so. There was no great speculation or borrowing, merely a hard-headed decision on where to go next. One of the great virtues of the travel agency business was that the customers' money was up front, perhaps by several weeks before it had to be passed on to the tour operator. Therefore, there were no bad debts. Once you had bought your property (Jim Moffat made it a business principle to be the owner) it was a case of opening shop and waiting to see if you had made the correct choice of location.

In his case, there was an extra dimension inasmuch as people began coming to him with the offer of their business for sale. Word had got around that Jim Moffat of Saltcoats was an honest man who would do a straight deal. Some of those potential sellers simply could not adjust to the new technology which had begun to creep in – and to the added competition which it had created. Others felt under pressure from the moans and groans of dissatisfied customers, who would bring their complaints to the travel agent, at the sharp end of the holiday industry, even if they had no control over whatever delay or disaster had ruined the annual fortnight in the sun. Some sellers had simply reached retirement age and wanted to see their carefully nurtured business pass into reliable hands. Jim Moffat was just such a man, an uncomplicated, friendly human being with whom they could discuss a possible transaction. Of course, he was no soft touch upon whom an ailing business could readily be unloaded but if it stood the test of its own criterion and fitted the pattern of his own expansionist thoughts, then he was more than willing to talk.

The early years, however, were not a period when expansion loomed large in the Moffat plans. It was much more important to consolidate what he had. From those two offices in Saltcoats and Kilmarnock, he added a very small travel agency, Nugent of Largs, which specialised in tours to Jersey and came his way in 1960 for the modest sum of £1,250.

In fact, it was ten years after starting out in business before he looked beyond his beloved Ayrshire and wondered if he would dare venture towards the metropolis of Glasgow. Someone had told him that the three best shopping streets in the city, outwith the central area, were Byres Road, in the West End, and Victoria Road and Shawlands Cross, on the South Side. Employing a method similar to Charles Forte, when he was trying to open his first milk bar in London, Jim Moffat went up Byres Road and undertook his own rather crude version of market research. He simply stood there, watching the flow of people and trying to assess how that would translate into customers deciding to book their holidays if he were to open shop there. One important factor seemed to be in his favour. As far as he could see, there was not another travel agent on Byres Road. His decision was made. This would be the first break into the big city, where the minnow from Saltcoats would compete for business with big fish like Thomas Cook. He managed to acquire a former carpet shop at the corner of Byres Road and Havelock

Street, opened up his travel shop – and was soon doing a brisk business which continues to this day, under the management of Jack Pullen, who carried off the special Branch of the Year award at the firm's 30th anniversary.

In that same year of Byres Road – 1965 – he bought a little company in Paisley called OSA Tours, which had a branch in Johnstone. The main thrust of the business was to do with that ruling whereby you had to be a member of a club to gain the advantage of cheaper charter travel. At OSA Tours they ran The Paisley Buddies Club, through a lady called Ma Broon, who made the arrangements, accompanied the groups to Canada or the United States, supervised their meetings and was not averse to a bit of old-fashioned discipline, on the lines of "Hey, yoose-yins at the back – shut up!" After ten years in business, therefore, Jim Moffat now had seven branches of A.T. MAYS and was beginning to feel confident in his judgment for choosing appropriate sites.

It was the mid-Sixties, a time of full employment and much affluence, when a great deal was happening in the economy of Scotland. It took only the first hint of a New Town being developed at nearby Irvine, with talk of a 200,000 population by the turn of the century, for Jim Moffat to acquire premises in the existing town's high street. He had already acquired a business in that other Ayrshire coastal resort of Troon, an old-established company run by a popular local character called Nessie Broon from Troon (Broons and A.T. MAYS seemed to go together!) who had sold leather goods on one hand and travel tickets on the other. Altogether the Sixties were beginning to swing into action at A.T. MAYS.

CHAPTER FIVE

The Clarkson Crash

THE decision to move into England had much to do with the Moffats' daughter Margaret, who had left Ardrossan Academy to join the business at Largs and then Saltcoats.

Margaret had been just old enough to remember her father's days in banking, though she was well shielded from his discontent there. A clearer memory was the excitement of her parents branching into business and to find that she could visit her mother in the old wooden shack and then cross over to the pet shop, a more interesting attraction for the child, where she would skip in after school and find her father at work with his sister Bessie. She would play at helping out in the pet shop and perhaps take home a puppy which was unwell. Tortoises used to be imported in containers from Turkey in those days and you would find them crawling all over the Moffat garden at Seafield Drive. (The import of tortoises is now banned.)

Margaret still has memories which range from her father trying to clip a restless Airedale Terrier, ending up with more blood than hair, to the day they opened ALL PETS – and she stood petrified by the spectacle of her little brother, Jamie, standing there with a live python wrapped round his neck! The opening ceremony had been performed by a well-known television personality of the time, George Cansdale, who worked with snakes. Jamie was then five and Margaret ten.

The Moffats' daughter, Margaret Borges.

THE CLARKSON CRASH

Her first move from Scotland came at the age of 18 when her workmate in the Largs branch, Anne Simmons, went off to work in London. Margaret decided to follow her, furnished with enough money from her father to last a month. The arrangement was that, if she had not found a job by then, she would return home. She arrived in London on the Friday and had found a job by the Monday, working for the travel company of Sapphire International, organising coach trips for American and Japanese visitors and private-car excursions to places like Stratford-upon-Avon.

Margaret met and married an Englishman, John Roe, and with house prices in London fairly prohibitive even then, they decided to move out to Colchester, which was still within commuting distance of her office in Baker Street. It was an exhausting routine, however, and Jim and Margie Moffat were concerned about her health when they visited Colchester and found her so thin. Jim went out for a walk around the town to think it over – and came back with a solution: "There must be room for another travel agency in Colchester," was his bright idea. It was primarily to accommodate his beloved daughter but, from such a personal consideration, the future shape of A.T. MAYS was fashioned.

They were moving into England for the first time and Margaret would be manager of the branch. For three years it was known as Kingsway Travel, to suit local knowledge, before it took on the parent name. Jim Moffat later struck on the wisdom of grouping his branches into regional clusters so he concentrated on that East Anglian area and, within a few years, had built up branches at Hadleigh in Suffolk, Seven Kings and Barkingside, Ilford, and in the up-market holiday resort of Frinton-on-Sea, over all of which Margaret became the regional manager. The English connection was building up nicely when suddenly there came a cruel blow.

Margaret remembers it well: "We had been doing tremendous business with Clarkson's, the Court Line tour operator, and we were in the local pub one night when I suddenly heard on the radio that the company had collapsed. I was in the office next morning by six o'clock and other members of the staff were arriving behind me, having heard the news and knowing how serious it was for us. I can still remember the old lady who had been a regular client of ours coming into the office at 11 o'clock, turned back from Gatwick with her suitcase. "What am I going to do?" she cried. What was she going to do indeed? It was the saddest day of my life and affected the staff very badly."

Margaret had to cope with customer backlash, a disspiriting experience not helped by difficulties in her own marriage. Subsequently divorced and re-married to a local architect, Andrew Borges, a Tory councillor in Colchester, she gave birth to their son, James Paul Borges, and resumed her career in the family firm. Her job of regional manager entailed much travelling and, once again, Margie Moffat was not too keen on her daughter driving up and down those increasingly hazardous English roads. When it became apparent she was doing justice to neither her family nor the business, she gave it up and has since devoted herself to the family, in their magnificent medieval house in Colchester. But she has never lost her sense of being part of A.T. MAYS and wouldn't miss the staff conferences, where she renews old friendships and maintains the connection.

Though the Clarkson experience can still haunt her, she has an abundance of happier memories, like the outings to ABTA conferences in Cannes, where she would join a group of carefree travel people at seafront restaurants, insisting on eating alfresco in the pouring rain, calling for umbrellas and finally convincing the French waiters that the British really are a crazy race.

CHAPTER SIX

Airlines and Hairlines

WITH his business now running successfully, Jim Moffat had the time to travel around the country and pinpoint likely locations – and back his judgment with a decision to open a shop. Of course there would be times when anticipation would come unstuck.

Rothesay people had a habit of crossing the Clyde estuary to book their holidays at the Largs branch but the attraction of the town as a new target for A.T. MAYS was heightened by the news that a community was to be created at nearby Portavadie to build platforms for the oil industry which had come to the North Sea. Sensing the prosperity of a boom-town, Jim Moffat opened a branch in Argyle Street, Rothesay, which still justifies itself even though the oil-rig project came to nothing in the end.

So the direction turned to Lanarkshire, in towns such as Motherwell, Wishaw and Coatbridge, with a purchase which proves how successfully the family of previous owners can become part of the wider enterprise. After the acquisition of Killop's Travel Agency in Coatbridge, the son and daughter-in-law of the family, David and Colina Killop, remained with A.T. MAYS and are today managers respectively of Glasgow's Alexandra parade and the Coatbridge branches. Even their daughter-in-law, Evelyn, has joined the staff and runs the Business Travel Centre in Royal Crescent, Glasgow.

Colina Killop of Coatbridge – first woman to head a branch.

AIRLINES AND HAIRLINES

The purchase of Solair Tours, in the traditional town of Greenock, and the opening of a kiosk in the burgeoning New Town of East Kilbride were further examples of the spectrum now embraced by A.T. MAYS. The kiosk, by the entrance to the bowling alley, was soon replaced by a thriving branch in the town's main Plaza.

By now, the original branch in the home-town of Saltcoats was bursting at the seams, acting not only as a branch in its own right but as the corporate head-quarters of A.T. MAYS. Clearly, new premises had to be found and there was great poignancy for Jim Moffat as he walked round to Nineyard Street, just as he had done for that daily money-exchange in his days as an unhappy bank clerk in the town. This time he had come as a confident, prosperous and thoroughly contented human being, intent on exchanging money for a vastly different purpose. By hand-ing over £25,000, he would become the proud owner of the old Royal Bank of Scotland in Saltcoats and transform it to become the headquarters of his blossom-ing business, with his own office within that part which was the manager's house.

The Royal Bank had opened up in the centre of Saltcoats and the premises in Nineyard Street had been lying empty for a time before Jim Moffat brought the old place, with its many memories, back to life. He also bought the nearby Conser-vative Club and linked them up with another building in between. Apart from relieving pressure on the Hamilton Street branch, that purchase also marked the 20th anniversary of the enterprise. By that watershed point at the turn of 1975–76, the Moffat family were now running exactly 20 branches of A.T. MAYS, a branch for every year of existence. That size of business was generating enough profit to finance a faster rate of growth – and that is exactly what began to happen in the latter part of the 1970s. Whereas it had taken those 20 years to reach as many branches, the next five-year period was to see that figure jump to 60, with a further 11 branches added in 1981.

Still the pattern was developing and the stories accumulating. The purchase of Travel Trek, in Springfield Road, Glasgow, brought the unwelcome discovery that the premises were riddled with rats, not that that presented any great hazard to Jim Moffat who had long since established himself as a heroic killer of vicious vermin from his original pet shop in Saltcoats! So the expansion went on, con-verting an old bank building in Duke Street, Glasgow, a gunsmith's shop in Cumnock.

Another breakthough seemed imminent when Jim Moffat bought over Brighter Holidays at 21 Royal Crescent, Glasgow, an in-set section of Sauchiehall Street's

49

western end. It extended the scope from travel agency to tour operator but that branch of the trade had become so fiercely competitive that the new acquisition fluctuated disconcertingly between profit and loss. After six years, he decided to sell it and had agreed a purchase price with Budget Holidays. Alas, that company went bankrupt before they had paid for it and Jim Moffat bought back the property from the Receiver, added the house next door – and Royal Crescent became a Business Travel Centre for A.T. MAYS, as well as the home of Air Savers, the bargain end of the company, dealing in flights only and cut-price offers made on a last-minute basis.

The fact that A.T. MAYS was now battling in the big league of British travel agencies did not preclude the power of the individual, as witness the purchase of the Pitt and Scott agency, just off St Enoch's Square in Glasgow. That firm happened to own a second branch, in Shettleston Road, which traded under its own name of George McClure Travel. George McClure turned out to be a popular character in Shettleston who, as well as being a Glasgow town councillor, ran a barber's shop – and sold airline tickets when he wasn't cutting hair. The value of George McClure's name in the local vicinity was obviously a matter of importance and Jim Moffat was shrewd enough not to disturb local loyalty. So he made his one exception as far as names were concerned and allowed the Shettleston branch to continue as George McClure Travel, as it does today, with the man himself still associated with the business. Thus Mr McClure has a privilege of public exposure which the boss of A.T. MAYS has denied to himself, albeit with the barber-shop element now removed. Outwith the business world, by contrast, there are still very few people who would know the name of Jim Moffat.

So the various strategies continued. When Grandfare opened their multi-franchise system in Cambridge Street, Glasgow, opposite the Hospitality Inn, A.T. MAYS moved in. A town-centre site near Gilmour Street Station, Paisley, cost £40,000. They followed population movements to housing schemes like Drumchapel and Pollok. They moved into Aberdeen, with its oil boom, and to Edinburgh and Dundee, through the purchase of the Scottish end of Frames' Travel, one of the oldest travel companies in Britain which, nevertheless, decided to shed its connection north of the border. That deal also gave A.T. MAYS a branch in Buchanan Street, Glasgow. Reminded of the value of shopping in Glasgow's Victoria Road and Shawlands Cross, they opened up in both streets.

Jim Moffat began to target county towns like Hamilton (opening up there cost him £90,000) and smaller towns like Girvan, which were not too near bigger centres like Ayr. He was looking at places with populations of 10,000 or more. He had never forgotten the story of MacDonald's, the famous hamburger company of America, which employed a hundred surveyors of likely sites. The rival Burger King evidently employed only three, who watched where MacDonald's were opening and followed them in! In a more modified way, Jim Moffat began to ask where Marks and Spencer was situated and knew that big stores like that do act as a public magnet with benefits for those who trade nearby. Again, it is more a matter of common sense than any profound business philosophy.

While believing basically that the cobbler should stick to his last, Jim Moffat strayed rather outwith his ken when he bought a Saltcoats garage which came on the market. As the previous owner pointed out, he was the best customer and could do worse than simply buy it over, which he did. So now there was A.T. MAYS MOTORS, along with the Mayfield Service Station, an Esso outlet in town. He also bought Burnside Coachworks at Kilwinning but has since sold that.

Back in the business he knows best, he was discovering the merits of business travel, providing a booking service on the doorstep of companies which needed a service. Thus you find A.T. MAYS with a desk at the headquarters of John Menzies in Edinburgh, at Collins Publishers, in Westerhill Road, Bishopbriggs, and at the IBM complex in Spango Valley, Greenock.

CHAPTER SEVEN

Expansion – At No Cost

BY 1982, A.T. MAYS had reached a total of 77 branches, from Aberdeen running down through Scotland to East Anglia and not far short of the Home Counties. But, if that seemed a healthy expansion in 27 years of business, the dawn of 1983 was to bring dramatic events which would double that number within a year.

For the explanation of that, we return to the 1959 story of how Jim Moffat acquired the single branch of Mays (Shipping and Travel) in Kilmarnock. The rest of that Kirkcaldy-based company was eventually bought out by another major business in the Fife town, the well-known linoleum company of Nairn and Williamson, who changed the name to Nairn Travel. The deputy chairman of Nairn and Williamson, Mr Brian Gilbert, was also chairman of Nairn Travel. In time, however, Nairn and Williamson was taken over by the giant Unilever, who decided that a travel business was not part of their profile. So Nairn Travel would have to go. This proved of interest to that same former chairman of the company, Brian Gilbert, who had by now moved on to become chief executive of the Dundee conglomerate of Low and Bonar. For a sum of £5.2 million, he brought his old company under the umbrella of his new one. Low and Bonar had substantial losses with their first year of Nairn Travel, however, and began to look around for a suitable point of merger. Who better than the man who had bought a single

53

branch of the original company back in 1959 and now, in 1983, was doing very well with his 77 branches around the country?

Thus, in a curious twist of business fate, Jim Moffat, who started his expansion through buying that Kilmarnock office of Mays (Shipping and Travel) nearly a quarter-of-a-century earlier, was now acquiring the entire business, albeit by the circuitous route of Kirkcaldy and Dundee. More precisely, he was taking a 70 per cent stake in the greatly enlarged A.T. MAYS group, which more than doubled its size at one fell swoop. Low and Bonar retained 30 per cent. With more than 140 branches now spreading across Britain, we come to the main explosion in the scale of A.T. MAYS.

Absorbing Nairn Travel into A.T. MAYS was achieved without any money changing hands so the Saltcoats firm had now reached beyond 140 branches without having incurred any borrowing at all. The fact that it was making profits of around £1 million in 1983 meant it could finance all normal expansion. Low and Bonar had found someone who could manage their business in a way they had not attained themselves and they were being given an initial 35 per cent shareholding in A.T. MAYS (convertible to 30 per cent) for what had already cost them £5.2 million.

Looking back on his thinking in the early 1980s, Jim Moffat says: "I had always had a great belief that you should do things on your own. But, in retrospect, the linking up with Nairn Travel was the smartest thing I ever did, doubling the size of the business without cost to myself.

"From them we acquired new management skills. Their senior staff were highly trained but they had gone through those lean periods of being taken over more than once, none of which had been much of a success, and now they were joining a company with a more assured future. I had wondered if getting involved with a public company would bring disciplines which would prove too much; but it was the best of all the moves."

In that first year of the new tie-up, A.T. MAYS continued to expand at a reasonable rate, adding 15 more branches in 1984. Low and Bonar, however, were keen to see the business expand more quickly and, if possible, for A.T. MAYS to become a public company so that they had a vehicle for getting back their investment. Anything which came on the market, therefore, was put under examination. The first major move in that direction came in November 1984, when the English-based travel agency of Hunting Lambert became available. This was a company which had started in the Newcastle area but spread south through

54

England and across to Wales. At the time of purchase, it was owned jointly by two public companies, the Hunting Group and Hill Samuel, the merchant bankers. Jim Moffat managed to buy out their 50 branches for £2.25 million and, on this occasion, he did have to borrow money for the first time. Whereas the acquisition of Nairn Travel had brought in an enthusiastic staff, the reception from the Hunting Lambert employees was of a different order. Having been under the wing of such a prestigious name as Hill Samuel, they were inclined to wonder what life would be like under this ambitious invader from north of the Scottish border. After all, this was Jim Moffat making his entrance to the London scene, inheriting offices in the City, Holborn and Sloane Street. Whereas the Scots company was well known within its own borders, it was still a little-known name in England, except in places like the Scots-populated town of Corby, where they had opened a desk in the local Asda store. Its name meant practically nothing in the metropolis itself.

In 1985, Jim Moffat cast his eye on the much smaller Bennetts of Edinburgh, which had six branches around the Dalkeith and Musselburgh areas. It was a family business where the parents had retired and the two sons wanted to get out. The price was £470,000. Again from the family business scene, they bought Grange Travel of Cumbria for £330,000 and ACT of Lancashire for £420,000, each with five branches.

Meanwhile, the Saltcoats firm had engaged a new chief executive, Sam Newlands, who had come from his job as financial director with Black and Edgington, formerly Black's of Greenock, the tent people. That company had under its wing Black's Travel Agency, with branches in Glasgow, Greenock, East Kilbride, Edinburgh and Dumfries and Mr Newlands found himself going back in 1987 to buy over the travel firm for his new employers, at a cost of £450,000. The other acquisition of 1987 was Jet Save Travel, with four branches in the Liverpool area, at a cost of £125,000.

So the expansion continued into 1988, which was another bustling time of buying over companies. In the summer came Deeside Travel, with 11 branches from Liverpool and Manchester down to Worcester (price £700,000), followed by Warner Travel of Cheltenham, with its eight branches in the Cotswolds (£240,000) and Welplanned Travel of Crewe (£130,000). Also in 1988 there were new openings at Kirby, Bishop Auckland, Oban, Fort William, Cowdenbeath, Stenhousemuir, Kirkintilloch, Penrith, Croydon, Slough and Swindon, taking the total to 272, with the plans to go beyond the 300 mark during 1989.

"What is happening in the travel trade towards the end of the 1980s," says Jim Moffat, "is that the one-man business is no longer able to compete with the big boys. We get invitations almost daily from people who would like to retire and want us to buy them out. It is tough and competitive and the big firms are winning. The smaller ones have been able to survive while the owners were young and active but even they are now finding it harder to cope. Until a few years ago, there was no discounting in the trade but now it is fiercely competitive."

With Low and Bonar egging him on to become a public company, for their own purposes, Jim Moffat had to take a long, hard look at the shape of things to come for A.T. MAYS. From that modest base of Saltcoats, which seemed to some people ridiculously off the beaten track, he surveyed the travel scene in which he was bobbing along with remarkable success, considering the scale of the opposition.

Leading the field was Thomas Cook, with 300 branches throughout Britain, and owned by the Midland Bank. Pickford's, once better known as furniture removers, were now on much the same scale as Thomas Cook, with 300 branches and the financial backing of the National Freight Corporation. Lunn Poly, again with around 300 outlets, was owned by the biggest of all tour operators, Thomson International. Competing for fourth place with A.T. MAYS was Hogg Robinson, another English company of comparable size. And here, having the audacity to bat in that premier league, was the Scottish firm from an Ayrshire holiday town.

It became more and more clear to Jim Moffat that decision time was fast approaching. He could go public, as Low and Bonar were suggesting, sell half his family stake in the company and feel very comfortably off for the rest of his days, while the other half would go to the expansion of A.T. MAYS. His aims, of course, were not the same as Low and Bonar's. But he was encouraged to go down that route in the belief that it would become more and more difficult to compete in the top league on equal terms.

As he was boiling up towards a decision in 1986, he was nevertheless deterred by the calculation that this would bring him only a few million pounds for a business which seemed worth much more. It was at that stage of doubt that fate took a hand, in the shape of approaches from two major institutions, the Royal Bank of Scotland and the Trustee Savings Bank. At first, Jim Moffat took a different line from the television commercial – and said "No" to both.

CHAPTER EIGHT

The Banks Who Said 'Yes?'

WHILE Jim Moffat was considering ways of financing further expansion – and flirting with the notion of putting A.T. MAYS on to the Stock Exchange as a public company – there were other forces at work which would decide his future.

Across in St Andrew Square, in the heart of Edinburgh, the board of the Royal Bank was turning its attention to a broader base of financial activity and the idea of buying over Scotland's biggest travel agency was high on the priority list. It all began with a phone-call to Jim Moffat from the chief executive of the Royal Bank, a jovial Dundonian called Charles Winter, a man who had worked himself up from bank-clerk level in his native city and, having relished his career much more than Jim had done in his own days behind the counter, reached quite spectacularly to the top of the tree. The phone-call was to the effect that he would like to meet Jim and Margie Moffat for dinner in Glasgow one evening, an invitation which was bound to arouse some curiosity as to what Mr Winter had in mind. Thus a big business deal begins.

But the background to the Royal Bank approach needs some examining on its own. The power to diversify had long been an option of British banks so it perhaps says a good deal about the sober-suited, fairly stodgy outlook of those austere institutions that for long enough they scarcely ventured outside a fairly limited field. A latent streak of enterprise in Scottish bankers, however, did show through

Charles Winter (right), Group Chief Executive of the Royal Bank of Scotland.

as far back as 1954 when the then chief executive of the Commercial Bank (later to be part of the Royal), Mr Ian MacDonald, led the way in introducing hire-purchase financing into British banking. But it took legislation in 1971 really to point the way for bankers to take a closer look at their traditional business and see if there were other forms of financing which might improve the return on the capital employed.

Until then banking had been very much a straight-forward business of taking deposits, with or without interest, and offering short-term overdrafts. The first moves after 1971 were to offer longer-term lending and to widen the range of deposit accounts, still very much within the traditional limits of the profession. The Royal Bank decided to offer services for which it could earn fees, irrespective of movement in interest rates. Today, that fee-earning capacity accounts for one-third of the bank's income. As the new departure gathered pace in the early 1970s, they expanded their hire-purchase financing and the leasing of equipment such as aeroplanes, most of which are owned not by the airlines but by the financial institutions.

They moved into plastic cards and, instead of acting as agents for other people's insurance business, decided to sell their own, bringing in a revolutionary new

The A.T. MAYS' operation board with Charles Winter (centre back, standing).

59

method of Direct Line insurance, which offered instant cover from a telephone call. The in-phrase now was "off-branch financing". The Financial Services Act of the 1980s gave added impetus to the trend and opened the way for the Royal to move into merchant banking, with the purchase of Charterhouse of London. That in turn opened the door to a stockbroking division, all of which would have been frowned upon not so long before. The view would have been that a retail bank, with its fiduciary responsibilities towards its depositors, should not be an investment bank, buying equity in other companies.

The Royal started a company called Royscot to handle those hire-purchase, leasing and fee-earning activities. The bank which had itself been the target of takeover not so long before, when the Hong Kong and Shanghai were the predators, was now looking outwards to doing business in other countries. And, in addition to all that, the directors were turning their thoughts to a travel agency, which they felt would take them to the very edge of financial services.

So what attracted them in this direction and to A.T. MAYS in particular? For a start, there was the fact that a travel agent sold travellers' cheques and foreign currency which, in the case of A.T. MAYS, was sometimes being provided by the bank itself. "I soon realised there was another attraction," said Charles Winter. "They had a big branch network in the high streets across the country and many of the services which we were selling, like insurance and other financial provisions, could just as readily be sold through a branch of A.T. MAYS. In buying them, we would be acquiring an extra 200 branches overnight – and that would take us into 70 locations where we were not represented at all. It was while doing our strategic planning in 1986, and trying to identify possibilities for the future, that we decided it would make sense to have a travel agency in the Royal Bank Group."

Thus the phone-call to the Moffats at their home in West Kilbride and that invitation to dinner in Glasgow. They turned up with no more than a suspicion of what was in the wind but Charles Winter soon put his cards on the table. "Wouldn't it be a good idea," he said, "to bring together Scotland's biggest and best bank and Scotland's biggest and best travel agency?"

It was a good tactical opening but Jim Moffat was not rushing into any agreement. Indeed, far from jumping at the idea, he told Charles Winter that, at first sight at least, his proposition did not really tie in with what he had in mind for the future of the company. "I suppose my ego was too strong," he now admits, "and I had cherished this pipe-dream of seeing the company I had founded being a listed share and that it would go on and on."

Winter was impressed by the fact that Moffat was mainly concerned about keeping faith with his staff and doing nothing which would jeopardise their position. In the passing, Jim Moffat did say he would sell them part of the company but the bottom line of Charles Winter's proposition was total acquisition of A.T. MAYS.

On reflection, of course, the founder's idea of floating the company on the Stock Exchange was much less of a guarantee to his staff than what Charles Winter had in mind. In dealing with the Royal Bank, he could at least lay down some conditions for teaming up, whereas an exposure to the Stock Exchange would lead to a loss of control altogether, perhaps ending up with A.T. MAYS being swallowed up by one of the bigger agencies, like Cook's, Lunn Poly or Pickford's. None of those would be likely to retain the name of A.T. MAYS or bother about a headquarters stuck away in a remote corner of Ayrshire. These were the sort of considerations at the back of Jim Moffat's mind. It would all take time to work out, however, and they agreed to finish their dinner and depart for some long, hard thinking.

The Royal's approach was not an entirely new idea. The Midland Bank had already bought Thomas Cook, adding the kind of financial clout which was going to be needed in the competitive world of travel.

Many months passed before the two men got together again. In the meantime, the Trustee Savings Bank, which had greatly heightened its profile by entering the public arena, cottoned on to the same idea as Charles Winter. "They made an approach but were rather dilatory about making up their minds," Jim Moffat recalls. "The Scottish end of the TSB were good enough to deal with but it was the London end that was sluggish."

Among the ironies of the matter, as he considered his various options, was the fact that the Royal Bank had once been bankers to A.T. MAYS but not any more. He had moved his account to the Bank of Scotland, which now found itself with a major client liable to be scooped away by its biggest rival. Its merchant banking wing, the British Linen, was not without its involvement, however, and Ian Brown, a very good friend and sound adviser to Jim Moffat, wanted to act as middle-man in any deal. "I turned him down," Jim Moffat says reflectively. "Perhaps I shouldn't."

By now, he had had experience of both the Royal and the TSB and was in no doubt as to which had the more professional approach. There was to be no turning back and he told the Royal he was ready to talk. At that stage, Charles Winter brought in another talented Scot, Robert Smith, from the merchant banking wing, Charterhouse. For a start, they would have to put down an indicative price on the table. Through all the hard-headedness of business deals, the final outcome can often depend on how the personalities involved get on with each other. Just as Jim Moffat had taken to Charles Winter, he found himself on the same wavelength as Robert Smith as well, each recognising in the other a straightforward kind of chap with whom you could deal fairly and reasonably.

Charles Winter noticed one other dimension to the discussions. He knew of Jim Moffat's days in the National Bank at Saltcoats (it would eventually become part of the Royal) and of his visits to the local branch of the Royal Bank for note exchange. Since he had bought that same branch to convert into his head-quarters, he betrayed to Winter a sign of emotion in the idea of completing the circle and returning to the bank which he had left as little more than a clerk. That had not been a particularly happy episode in his life but there was surely now a special irony in the situation, especially when that return would very quickly make him a multi-millionaire! All else being equal, Charles Winter thought, Jim Moffat would choose to team up with the Royal Bank of Scotland.

The procedure of takeover was followed through in the normal way, with more and more advisers brought to the table until they had reached a point of agreement. All was more or less signed and sealed, though not legally so, when the TSB suddenly showed an urgency which had been lacking in its previous overtures. It came up with an offer to beat the Royal Bank's one but it arrived just as Jim Moffat was leaving for Edinburgh to sign over A.T. MAYS to the Royal Bank.

Here was the dilemma of anyone faced with a better offer which they are entitled to accept. More money was on the table, yet he had come a long way with the men of the Royal for whom he had now gained the highest respect. He hastened to Edinburgh and told them what had happened. Charles Winter conceded that, while he would be sad to see him go to the TSB, he was still legally entitled to do so. He was counting on Jim Moffat's adherence to a gentlemen's agreement and, on that score of conscience alone, he was on safe ground.

Jim Moffat took a leaf out of his other suitor's book and said "Yes" to the Royal, which immediately gained a majority stake in A.T. MAYS, buying 58 per cent for £9.8 million. The remainder of the company was set on a course of purchase over five years, from 1987 until 1992, with Jim Moffat remaining as chairman till then and his final buy-out figure being related to performance. The company had

had two particularly good years before the deal and the bank was not anxious to pay a price which was based on those two years alone. It is in the modern way of things that people bought out are often given the responsibility of proving that their recent performances can be continued into the future.

In preparing to collect a final sum which was likely to be no less than £18 million, the former bank clerk stuck to his two conditions. The retention of the company name presented no problems at all. Indeed it would have been foolish for the bank to tamper with such an established title. On the question of keeping the headquarters in Saltcoats, where it was such an important means of local employment, Charles Winter gave another assurance that he was not in the business of tampering with that, even if Saltcoats was not the easiest place in the world to reach! Some banking people would have to come from London to board meetings in the Ayrshire resort and they would certainly have preferred their destination to be Glasgow. If Jim Moffat had felt disposed to moving it, Charles Winter would have been happy to do so. But it was not a point of argument and he gave a categorical assurance, not only to Jim but to the local MP, Mr Brian Wilson, who was quickly on the phone, full of concern about loss of jobs in the area.

The presence of Jim Moffat as chairman until 1992 was a guarantee in itself up to that point. The bank is unlikely to feel bound in perpetuity by the conditions and it remains to be seen what happens after the retirement of Charles Winter in 1993. The name of A.T. MAYS is unlikely to be bettered, being short, simple and easily marketed. The most that can be said at the time of this book, two years after the deal, is that no one at the bank has talked in any serious way about changing either the name or the headquarters.

Charles Winter felt his own attachment to the headquarters in Saltcoats, having visited the branch regularly in his days as an inspector and remembering clearly, if not the manager's face, at least the form of his signature. In considering his new purchase, he knew there was one other advantage in being the owners of A.T. MAYS. Whereas it cost a bank upwards of £500,000 to open a new branch, a travel agency could do it for a mere £50,000. On top of that, local authorities were not always well disposed to a bank opening up on the high street since they were concerned about the disappearance of shop fronts.

As far as the future was concerned, the bank had nothing in mind except expansion, continuing to open branches in the pattern which Jim Moffat had already established, especially in areas where they themselves were not represented, and to have more and more selling of Royal Bank services.

In the way that such deals are concluded, Jim Moffat would normally have become a director of the Royal Bank, as indeed he would have wished. But Sir Michael Herries, chairman of the Royal, had been pursuing a policy of younger directors and such an appointment would have flown in the face of all he had been preaching. Jim Moffat was already 68. Instead, he was appointed a director of Royscot, the offshoot financial group which had its headquarters in Cheltenham – one of the reasons A.T. MAYS decided to buy Warner Travel in that same town.

Under the new set-up, there is an A.T. MAYS Group plc, which is the top decision-making board for all that happens in the company. It consists of Jim Moffat as chairman, along with his chief executive, Sam Newlands, his son Jamie, who is managing director, his wife Margie, Alan Bromfield, the deputy managing director, and directors of the Royal Bank: James Greer, James Rafferty, Robert Smith, Bob Riding and Dr Ian Dugdale. Then comes A.T. MAYS Ltd, the board which carries out the executive decisions. That consists of chairman Jim Moffat, Sam Newlands, Jamie Moffat, Alan Bromfield, financial director Gordon Pattison (he came with Hunting Lambert), personnel director Lindsay Grattan, Margie Moffat and Jim Rafferty of the bank.

That financial deal with the Royal Bank took place in November 1987, since when Jim Moffat has continued doing much as before, leading the business from the front and knowing that performance is still of vital importance, not only to determine his final pay-out but to fulfil his moral obligation.

Looking back on the decision to sell, he reassures himself with the thought that his conditions have been met, with guarantees as good as you can ever achieve. In retrospect, he can now say: "While there are no regrets, I do occasionally think to myself that it will never be quite the same again. It used to be a one-man band in which I called the tune and made all the decisions.

"But, in other respects, it is a relief. We needed the backing of a highly respected financial institution and we found it in the Royal Bank of Scotland. They approached us in a very gentlemanly way and there was an immediate chemistry between Charles Winter and myself.

"In the first year together, we opened 35 branches, which would not have been possible from our own resources. We might have been thinking about ten. The importance of keeping the base in Saltcoats can be seen from the fact that we employ 300 of our 2,200 staff there. With firms like the Nobel Division of ICI cutting back, we had created employment in an area which badly needed it."

There were also reciprocal advantages between the respective staffs. Bank employees, for example, were now entitled to travel concessions. Other advantages to A.T. MAYS included a smartening up of accounting procedures and access to the bank's internal mail system, which proved invaluable during the postal strike of 1988. The link-up had the additional value of spreading the name into corners of England where the company was little known.

As Jim Moffat settled down to that agreement of remaining as chairman, there was just one cloud on the horizon, a matter much discussed in the travel trade during the late 1980s. It was the sudden and explosive expansion of Lunn Poly, which had usually taken second place to Thomas Cook. Within a year, they opened more than one hundred new branches and raised questions in the trade about what was in the mind of their owners and masters, Thomson, the biggest tour operator in the world. There was an obvious danger that, if Lunn Poly could sell enough Thomson holidays through the firm's own retail outlet, the others who deal with Thomson might dwindle in importance. It certainly meant that Thomson had, at their fingertips, all the statistics of Lunn Poly's rivals – Cook's, Pickford's, A.T. MAYS and Hogg Robinson – and would know what they were achieving by comparison. That scenario had not escaped the Royal Bank either and Charles Winter conceded that he had expected more time to adjust to the possibility than experience had allowed, while at the same time making it plain he was not unduly worried. One of the bank's aims had been to enable A.T. MAYS to establish a bigger and better business travel arm, not only for improving revenue but for that purpose of making them less dependent on the tours which came from the big operators.

Keeping matters in perspective, he could point to the fact that, in the overall picture of the Royal Bank Group, the travel agency contributed £2 million to the group profits of £309 million in 1988 and that a setback would therefore not be disastrous. Nevertheless, he made it plain that he would be sad if A.T. MAYS did not grow and prosper as intended.

He is impressed by Jim Moffat's record and the fact that he has employed good quality people, who know their business and run it in a thoroughly professional manner. Charles Winter also noted that Jim Moffat had not forgotten his own bank training and would scribble away on his pad very shrewdly.

In terms of straightforward competition, Jim Moffat had nothing to fear from anyone. With that excellent track record, he kept forging ahead under the new set-up, showing the same interest, loyalty and determination which encouraged him to leave the bank counter in the first place and test himself out in the hurly-burly of business. He has gradually adjusted to the change of ownership but manages to retain that sense of family business. He prides himself in being the only person around who still goes round his premises putting out unnecessary lights and picking up pins!

CHAPTER NINE

Where is Saltcoats?

IF the town of Saltcoats has benefited from the employment provided by A.T. MAYS, it could also be excused if it has developed an inferiority complex from the publicity surrounding its role as the headquarters of that local firm. Even within these pages we have reiterated the notion of a small-town backwater, an eccentric location for the headquarters of one of Britain's major travel companies. In the madness of the modern world, we expect everything to be centralised in London, Birmingham, Manchester, Glasgow or Edinburgh so that the hard-pressed businessman, with bulging brief-case and furrowed brow, can shuttle from point to point and back in a day for some overall purpose which might include a bigger ulcer and a clotted artery.

There is no reversing of the trend, of course, but in this relentless drive of progress it does make for pleasant contemplation to find such an important company maintaining its real base in the place where it began. Many another company would simply keep a token presence there and move the seat of actual power to the bigger centre. But Saltcoats has remained the home and headquarters of A.T. MAYS for more than 30 years and those in search of the boss have had to prise themselves out of their familiar routes and negotiate winding by-ways of rural Ayrshire, which can have done them nothing but good.

So what kind of a town is it, this Saltcoats by the sea, which has been much maligned by those who don't know any better?

The seafront at Saltcoats, home of A.T. MAYS.

It is a douce little town on that Ayrshire coast, forming a kind of three-part conurbation with the neighbouring communities of Ardrossan and Stevenston, lying in the centre of that arrangement and gaining focus as the main shopping centre of it. Like several Ayrshire towns, not much of its appearance falls into any predictable pattern of street planning, a feature which adds to its charm if not to the ease of the visitor in finding his way around. There are sudden twists and turns, rises and falls, which make you feel that these are not the kind of streets you have encountered before.

It is on one such twist and turn that you come upon the original sites of the ALL PETS and ALL TRAVEL shops of James Moffat, situated within a hundred yards of each other, the pets in Chapelwell Street and the travel in Manse Street. The pet shop had been an electrician's and the wooden hut which first housed the fledgling travel business was formerly the premises of Reid the Undertaker, situated conveniently across the street from the local graveyard, with Saltcoats railway station just behind.

WHERE IS SALTCOATS?

A short-cut through the cemetery takes you on to Hamilton Street, the second street of Saltcoats, which was where Jim Moffat found premises suitable to accommodate both his businesses next door to each other. They are still there today, an A.T. MAYS travel shop with the ALL PETS next door, no longer owned by the Moffats but standing as a reminder of simpler days.

From Hamilton Street you walk a short distance to the town centre and cross into the main thoroughfare which has now been turned into a pedestrian precinct in the familiar fashion. You may find it bustling with shoppers while, left and right, there are alleyways ready to surprise you. Dart along one of those lanes and you are liable to find yourself on the seafront which helped to put Saltcoats high on that list of familiar names which formed the destinations of those Glasgow people who came "doon the watter" for their summer holidays. A churning, broken sea reminds you that this was once balm to those city folks who came from their smoke-ridden slums in days gone by, welcoming the chance to breathe a sea air which was at least fresh and bracing, even if it lacked the warmth of more southern parts. Given the sunshine to which A.T. MAYS now despatches the multitude, Saltcoats itself would be an appealing holiday town, with its long, curved beach and friendly Ayrshire folk to play host. In its day, it was a kind of summer holiday Mecca for those who faced west.

As you saunter down that main thoroughfare, you run into the irony that a prime shopping site in Saltcoats is occupied by none other than Hogg Robinson, one of A.T. MAYS' rivals in the big five of Britain's travel retail trade. If that sticks in the thrapple of the man who gave his home town a national company, it is explained by the fact that two of his employees left to open their own travel business in town, acquired that central site – and later sold out to the rivals of their former employer. Such is business. Another employee left to start his own travel shop and he, too, competes with his former employer in the heart of the Ayrshire town. A.T. MAYS still claim to out-perform the joint businesses of the local rivals but Jim Moffat concedes that there are ambitious young people with the same kind of aspirations as he himself harboured in his days as a disgruntled bank clerk and who feel that they can follow his example.

The reality is that these aspiring business people of the 1980s have faced a competitive environment which is far more testing than that encountered by the young Moffat in 1955. As in other areas of life, the movement has been towards bigger units, encouraged by the dependence on a computerised system of booking.

'TIS BETTER TO TRAVEL

So A.T. MAYS has spawned its own local rivals, in the traditional manner of the enterprise culture. Meanwhile, Saltcoats basks in the reflected glory of the company which put its name on the map – and sent countless people scurrying towards that map to find where it is, and how to get there.

CHAPTER TEN

Guest of Honour

IF the story so far has dealt mainly with the anatomy of a Scottish company, how it was founded, became established and grew to national proportions, the deeper dimension of the tale has to do with the people who have made it work.

Charles Winter was instantly impressed by the calibre of people employed by A.T. MAYS, a matter which generally tells you a great deal about the man at the top. It may seem like a minor point but you learn much about a company from the attitude of that first receptionist who answers your telephone call. Even then, one sometimes wonders how people at the top can possibly encompass their vast organisations and feel that they have any real sense of overall control. How do they know that employees are working in their employer's best interests and so on?

Lord Beaverbrook, a shrewd observer of the human race, put it simply. Give him any group of a hundred people, he said, and he would divide them into ten groups of ten, with a boss in each group. Appointing one boss over the ten bosses, he could then walk away and feel that the system would look after itself. There is a lot of truth in that, as his own employees in Scotland can testify from those days when the *Daily Express* employed 2,000 people north of the border. Lord Beaverbrook dropped in one day in 1941, while on his way to the Hebrides as Minister of Aircraft Production during the war – and they didn't see him again until 1961! For 20 years, the system spun along splendidly without his presence,

71

thousands of people coming and going, succeeding, failing, rejoicing, sweating and maybe even dying for a man they didn't see.

Like many another boss, Beaverbrook knew that he had given a structure of living to many people and that they would act out their role in the knowledge that they were serving the interests of both Beaverbrook and themselves which were, in fact, inseparable. If they were not doing so, the system would soon find them out.

Even within the decency of Ayrshire folk, Jim Moffat soon found that there were those who tried to beat the system, a matter to which we shall return at a later stage. But with the vast majority, he had chosen well and built around him a structure of people who liked and respected the man and felt that, in joining A.T. MAYS, they had become part of a family. So the flesh and blood of this story rests very much with the individuals and it is through those individual cases that a clearer picture of a company's history really emerges.

Of all the thousands of people who have worked for A.T. MAYS over the years, a certain pride of place goes to an Ayrshire farmer's wife who can claim to have been the very first person employed by the Moffats when they opened their ALL TRAVEL business in Saltcoats in the mid-1950s. It was perfectly fitting that, when A.T. MAYS held its 25th anniversary, the Guest of Honour that night should be the former Minnie Kerr, now Mrs Robbie Chalmers from the farm of Little Ittington, Ardrossan. When Minnie Kerr took up her job as clerkess in that wooden hut in Manse Street, Saltcoats, she faced not just the challenge and excitement of her first day as a working girl. It was also the final victory in her fight with the crippling disease of poliomyelitis, which struck her down in 1940, at the age of three.

Little was known about polio 50 years ago and, as in many other cases at that time, there was delay in diagnosing what was wrong. There followed long spells in Yorkhill Hospital for Sick Children in Glasgow and, when she developed a limp in the weakend leg, there were further spells in Killearn Hospital, where her good leg was shortened to help match the other one. All that meant serious interruption to her schooldays though, with characteristic courage, she fought her way back to fitness, completed her schooling at Ardrossan Academy and ended up as sports captain of the school, playing volleyball and keeping goal for the hockey team. Her father, an ICI chemist who came of farming stock, had moved the family from Stevenston to Saltcoats and it was a neighbour in Eglinton Street who mentioned her name to Mr and Mrs Moffat, just as they were looking for their first employee.

Minnie Kerr (now Mrs Chalmers) – first ever employee of A.T. MAYS.

Minnie Kerr went in to work on Saturday mornings at first but, when she left school in 1956, she joined as the very first person to be engaged by the firm. She remembers it well: "I joined Margie Moffat in that wooden hut in Manse Street and, believe me, it really was a wooden hut, with a front shop and a wee place at the back.

"I did everything from filling in booking forms to typing letters and making the tea. I also did the letters for the pet shop across the road. Mrs Moffat and I continued on our own till we were joined by the second employee, Margaret Teevan, and her arrival enabled me to be more on the counter. Having been in a wheelchair during my childhood, I was just glad to be settling into my first job. But none of us had any experience of the travel business.

73

'TIS BETTER TO TRAVEL

"They had applied for a railway ticket agency and Mr Moffat had told Margie and I that, when we reached £100 of railway business in a week, he would take us to dinner. I kept selling daily and weekly tickets, Margie dealt with the monthly returns and I can still recall the excitement of that week when we reached the figure. True to his word, Mr Moffat took us up to Glasgow for dinner and we ended the evening at the theatre, hearing the well-known singer of the day, the late Michael Holliday.

"I remember booking my very first continental holiday for a local couple who wanted to go to Paris for their honeymoon. They were a Mr and Mrs Ryland – I still see Mrs Ryland around Saltcoats today – and I was so relieved when they came in on their return to say the arrangement had gone so well and that they had arrived home safely. In those early days of foreign travel we took it all so personally, hoping that everything would go well and feeling so elated when the customer came in to confirm that it had. It was all such a challenge to us, every booking an adventure.

"We would make the actual booking by telephone and follow it up with a letter of confirmation. We dealt with Glasgow companies like Scotia, Cotter's and Brighter Holidays as well as the southern companies like Thomas Cook, Lunn Poly and Horizon. There was not a great deal of continental travel but people like Cotter's did have a bus tour to Austria and the Swiss lakes which was very popular.

"I must say that running a travel shop and a pet shop seemed an unlikely combination but Jim and Margie Moffat worked tremendously hard and Mr Moffat was making a huge success of the pets business. From time to time he would pop over to see how we were doing, leaving his sister Bessie in the pet shop. He might come for a cup of tea, then, if things were quiet, Margie would pop out to do her shopping.

"It was as informal as that, with a real friendly atmosphere, and when you consider on how small a scale we were working, it is all the more astounding that A.T. MAYS has grown to the size it is today. I find it hard to believe. Then the two businesses came side by side in Hamilton Street and I remember, when they made their first move towards expansion by taking over the Mays branch in Kilmarnock, Mr and Mrs Moffat and myself were discussing what they should call the enlarged business, in order to keep the identity.

"Small incidents stick in your mind. I can still recall the lady who came into the Hamilton Street shop one day to book a holiday to Canada. She wanted to pay for her flight in cash and proceeded to put down those enormous, old-fashioned

GUEST OF HONOUR

white notes which had clearly come from under the bed and were smelling of mothballs. I had never seen that kind of currency before and rushed to find Mrs Moffat and bring her to the counter to verify that they were all right!"

Minnie Kerr left A.T. MAYS in 1960 to marry Robbie Chalmers, who was farming at Little Ittington, the neighbouring place to his childhood home of Muirlaught Farm at Saltcoats. Throughout her busy life as a farmer's wife, however, she has never lost contact with the Moffats and still takes a real pride in that business whose roots she helped to establish. In the early days of her marriage, you would find her coming into Saltcoats for a chat and cup of coffee with Margie and delivering eggs for the Moffats and other members of the staff.

No wonder Jim and Margie chose her for that Guest of Honour spot when it came to the company's silver anniversary. For Minnie Kerr represented that kind of solid, decent, dependable and courteous employee the Moffats were looking for in establishing their small family business. Having set an example and precedent in the calibre of their staff, they knew what standards should be maintained as the growth of A.T. MAYS began to take root.

So how does it seem now to Minnie as she tells her three sons about the firm she joined as a girl in the mid-1950s?

"I think it's just wonderful that, from such a modest beginning in this wee provincial town, the firm has grown to be so big and successful. The Moffats worked hard in those early days and deserve their success, for it was no easy matter. You had to prove to people like the Association of British Travel Agents that you were worthy of their membership.

"On the personal level, what amazes me is that they have remained the same unspoiled people I knew in the beginning. Success hasn't changed them in the slightest. I think Margie intended to work until the business got off the ground but here she is, all these years later, still working and enjoying it.

"As for Jim, he takes the same pride and satisfaction from doing things as well as he possibly can. Obviously, the more exciting developments happened after I left but I am just proud to have been part of the beginning, to have worked there when nobody had any idea of what lay in the future. I still feel myself very much a part of what happens in the business which Jim and Margie Moffat started all those years ago."

In the days of Minnie Kerr, the biggest rush was the Glasgow Fair, when the whole of Glasgow, it seemed, was going by bus or train to either Blackpool or to Butlin's at Skegness. That was the week they ran their marathon in the Scottish

75

A.T. MAYS *office party, 1962.*

travel trade and Jim Moffat would see the last of them off then order a party for
his staff. In those early days that was a fairly simple task. There was just a handful
of people, based in Saltcoats, so they all came along to the Moffat home in
Ardrossan for a meal and some music and they all let their hair down for the night.
Another milestone had been reached in the fledgling business and they were glad
to have served their public and seen them off on their annual outing. In time,
of course, there were too many people to invite to the house so Jim and Margie
took them to the Eglinton Hotel in Ardrossan. It is part of the price of expansion
when you get as big as A.T. MAYS that there wouldn't be a hotel big enough
to accommodate the entire staff and that much of that intimacy among staff is
bound to diminish.

  The format nowadays is that everyone from branch manager level upwards
gathers at the Hospitality Inn, Glasgow, once a year for a two-day conference.
That means around 400 people turning up to discuss policy, to review the year

just gone and put forward ideas for the year ahead. Starting on the Saturday lunch-time, they confer all afternoon and end the day with a dinner in the evening. The same happens on the Sunday before they disperse to the four winds. To keep in touch with the rest of their staff, Jim and Margie Moffat made it a habit, until 1987, to visit every area once a year. They would take all staff in that area out to enjoy a meal together and get to know about their families. That becomes less and less possible as expansion continues but they still pay periodic calls, especially where new branches have been opened and they may be meeting some of their staff for the first time.

In a quickly changing world, there is just a hint of regret as Jim Moffat tells you about those modern methods of communication which have replaced the human contact. Apart from sophisticated computers, they now have facsimile machines, telex and Midas – and they talk to a mysterious lady called Iris, which is the codename for the booking operation. She's a pretty fast lady, high-stepping and efficient. But she doesn't have half the good looks or the charm of a warm-hearted human like Minnie Kerr!

CHAPTER ELEVEN

All the Macmillans

IT is interesting to trace the origins of the people who found their way into A.T. MAYS and made a career of it. A case in point is that of a man with the colourful Viking-Scottish name of Somerled Macmillan, whose connection with the firm is quite unique.

Bred from South Uist people, Erl Macmillan, as he came to be known, was brought up in Fife and left school to become a railway clerk. Looking for a change of direction after National Service, he called at the Labour Exchange in Kirkcaldy to see what jobs were in prospect. There was nothing at the moment, said the man, and Erl was leaving when the voice at the counter called him back. He had just remembered hearing indirectly that Mays, the shipping people, were needing somebody, if that interested him. He went along, was interviewed by Mr McGlashan and landed the job, largely on the strength of his railway experience. But he could hardly have anticipated what he was starting, not only for himself but for most of his family. For the Macmillan saga today is a family story within the family story of A.T. MAYS. It reached a stage where ten members of Erl's family were working for the company, giving rise to the joke that the much-used initials of A.T.M. did not so much stand for A.T. MAYS as All The Macmillans!

Joining the original Mays company in 1957, at the age of 25, Erl was sent westward to the Kilmarnock office, where they had been having some staffing

Somerled Macmillan – first of "all the Macmillans".

problems. His arrival reinforced the Kirkcaldy element on the staff, who were generally referred to, no doubt with some sarcasm, as "The three wise men from the East". There was a Kirkcaldy way of doing things as opposed to the Kilmarnock way and the incomers were seen to be putting across the company policy. About a year after his arrival, however, ownership switched from Kirkcaldy to Saltcoats, just down the road from Kilmarnock. Jim Moffat had bought that one branch of Mays.

Erl was already married to Margaret, who was to join him in the Kilmarnock branch, where he became manager in 1966. Of their five sons, one is an accountant in Abu Dhabi and another is with the TSB. But the three others all followed their father and mother into the travel empire of A.T. MAYS. David is retail sales manager at head office, Robert is regional manager in Aberdeen and Donald is branch manager in Stranraer. But it doesn't end there. Erl's brother Bob became branch manager at Glenrothes, back in their native Fife. Then came the daughters-in-law. Robert's wife, the former Linda Ferguson from Saltcoats, went to work at Asda's in-store branch of A.T. MAYS in Aberdeen. Donald's wife, Linda Galloway from Kilmarnock, was in the Stranraer branch before leaving to have her family. David's wife, the former Irene Fulton, became assistant manager at Bank Street, Kilmarnock, where life could become rather confusing. Erl's wife, Margaret, is now cashier there and there was one stage when a customer calling to ask for "Mrs Macmillan" had a choice of no fewer than four! So that added up to nine people with the name of Macmillan from the one family, plus Irene's brother-in-law, Martin McCutcheon, another branch manager.

For Erl Macmillan, by now regional manager for Ayrshire and south-west Scotland and in a position to recommend appointments, it was often a difficult decision between being accused of nepotism and being fair to members of his own family, who were genuinely interested in following the parents into A.T. MAYS.

Anyway, he is substantial enough to withstand criticism, a stocky anchor-man who quickly came to appreciate the advantages of the new ownership of Jim Moffat. Though the company would grow to be a multiple, it was to retain the family atmosphere so rare in big business, with the staff so regularly and personally in contact with the Moffats.

"Though it is not necessarily the same now," said Erl Macmillan, "it was a lot of fun in the early days. When the firm was smaller, there was plenty scope for a social life, annual dances, 21st birthday parties and so on. The dominant feature was always the strong personality of Jim Moffat himself.

"Nowadays this business is more competitive and you work hard to achieve results. A feature of earlier times was when Mr Moffat used to hire the Isle of Man steamer and take people on the crossing from Ayr to Belfast for the day. That was before the troubles in Northern Ireland.

"We used to have our own jargon, developed largely from phrases used by the boss himself. If someone in the company was showing promise they would become known as "one for the future". Someone not making the grade became "an average performer". He would remind us managers that we were virtually "running your own business", which was his way of giving people a sense of their own responsibility.

"The mail-run on a Tuesday became a feature of life in the early days. That meant the Moffats themselves would deliver memos personally, making it an occasion to visit the various branches. That way the boss felt he could gauge very well what was happening in the company.

"This job certainly gets you around a bit. In the early days, believe it or not, I went to Lebanon. I have also been to Japan, via Bangkok, as well as Russia and South Africa. Just recently, my wife and I took a group to the Caribbean. The travel trade gets a hold of you to the point that, after a while and despite its problems, you don't see yourself doing anything else. The continuity of employment has also been good for people. That feeling of family with the company has been so strong that, if I had ever been thinking of leaving, it would almost have been like leaving home."

How did the staff react when they heard about the Royal Bank buy-out?

"We thought it would never happen to us and some of the staff got quite a shock," he admits. "But at least the shock was tempered by the fact that we were being taken over by a Scottish bank and that seemed better than someone like Lunn Poly. The Royal seem to have no desire to take over the running of the agency and we are still left to get on with it. We display their Access leaflets on the counter and our financial year has changed to coincide with the bank's but, apart from that, we know little difference. At least the bank staff know who we are. When we took over Hunting Lambert in England, their staff wondered where they were going. There had been rumours in London that they were being taken over by Thomas Cook but, when they heard it was A.T. MAYS, their first question was 'Who is A.T. MAYS?' "

But what about that name of Somerled Macmillan?

"I have spent my life trying to explain it to people. I wished at first that I had been born plain John Smith. My parents shortened it to Erl but many people called me 'Mac', though I found that became mistaken for 'Mark'. Still, I came to the conclusion that, if Peregrine Worsthorne of the *Sunday Telegraph* could live with a name like that, I shouldn't be grumbling about Somerled Macmillan!''

Somerled, who lives in Prestwick, makes this assessment of Jim Moffat: "Basically, what he seems to have is charm, that ability to get people to do things. Whether you agree with him or not, he can make it seem like the right thing to do. People lay a great deal of store on what he says. Sometimes I have argued with him and indicated that there was a 'Saltcoats factor' at work. One colleague used to claim there were three parts of A.T. MAYS – Saltcoats, Largs and the rest of the United Kingdom! Mr Moffat was once in the bank in Largs and we used to think he had a sympathy for that area, as well as for Saltcoats, where it all started. If something happened in Saltcoats, it would be worse than if it happened anywhere else – or so we thought!

"As far as having headquarters in Saltcoats was concerned, it was generally felt at one time, perhaps within the trade, that we were not taken seriously enough because we didn't have our headquarters in Glasgow, where people expected us to be. It must have given an impression of being parochial. But we did get bigger and eventually the critics just fell by the wayside. There was certainly a time when we tended to feel too much in awe of the big names in travel.

"To show how much things have changed, I remember visiting Mr Moffat in Saltcoats in the early 1960s, when his office was in the pet shop and the travel was just a sideline next door. We were suddenly interrupted by a phone call and there he was, taking an order for a goldfish and some cat-meat! He was also giving me a kitten for the family."

From such beginnings a business grew. Little wonder that Clan Macmillan appreciate that day when Somerled heard a voice at the Labour Exchange counter – and went back to see what it was all about.

CHAPTER TWELVE

The Man Who Lost His Trousers

LINDSAY GRATTAN has risen to be personnel director of A.T. MAYS but still marvels that he got anywhere, considering a rather inauspicious start with the company.

Born and brought up in Troon, he left school in 1962, looked around for work, without success, and went one day to seek a post as a trainee accountant. He didn't get the job but just as he was leaving (and not unlike the experience of Somerled Macmillan) the man suddenly remembered that he had heard of someone looking for a travel clerk.

It was a bleak, wet winter day when Lindsay Grattan turned up for his interview, arriving so early that he walked up and down and was thoroughly soaked by the time he was shown in to see Mr Moffat. He recalls doing nothing in the interview to justify his selection but felt the boss was so sorry for the bedraggled lad that he took pity on him and gave him the job. It could well be true. Yet, by such fickle fortune, Jim Moffat found his future director of personnel.

The vacancy was at Bank Street, Kilmarnock, but when Lindsay turned up to start work that Monday morning he found the place had been bulldozed for renovation. There was just a hole in the floor and the staff were working from a cellar which was supported by a telegraph pole. What's more, with the power cut off, they were working by the light of candles – and the snow was coming!

Lindsay Grattan, Personnel Director.

From scenes like these, however, Lindsay became manager at Irvine and then at the second location in Kilmarnock, in King Street. A national power strike and a three-day working week were to play another fortuitous part in his career. With business suffering as a result, managers were encouraged to do other things. Lindsay Grattan was among those who took up the training of staff and found that he had a natural aptitude for it. Once the power strike was over, he was given the job of training officer, a role which expanded suddenly in 1983 when Nairn Travel came under the wing of A.T. MAYS and the staff numbers went up from 300 to 800. Thus he became personnel and training officer and finally personnel director. Today he deals with no fewer than 2,240 staff members, their appointments, transfers, replacement, maternity leave and so on, as well as more than 200 entrants from the Youth Training Service, with whom A.T. MAYS has one of the highest success rates in the travel trade. Of the youngsters who arrive under the YTS scheme, upwards of 85 per cent remain on the staff and the ones who leave tend to do so by their own volition, having realised themselves that they are not cut out for it. The present YTS scheme was preceded by what was known as the Work Experience Programme and, out of those two schemes, there are already young people who have become branch managers by the time they had reached their early twenties.

Jim Moffat is delighted with the level of attainment in the YTS programme, as indeed he might well be. There has been much criticism of the scheme, often branded as a means of cheap labour, by which companies employ the youngsters for that minimum period, during which they are paid by the Government, before switching to a new and less expensive batch. No such situation exists at A.T. MAYS. Having undergone their college training in selling, communications, geography and so on, along with work experience in a branch, they have generally reached such a level of competence that the company is glad to have them on the staff.

The youngsters arrive under the ABTA scheme and are guaranteed the day-release required to follow through the courses. The college courses in Glasgow, Dundee and Lancaster are actually run for A.T. MAYS pupils exclusively and that training includes a trip abroad, culminating in a prize-giving at the end of two years, by which time they have donned the company uniform. Apart from the minority who realise that their talents could be better employed elsewhere, the young entrants quickly recognise that this is something far removed from the hum-drum jobs to which many of their friends are committed – and there is a determination to prove themselves capable of making it their career.

Many of the girls who join A.T. MAYS eventually leave to have family but once the children are off their hands, they are anxious to resume work, perhaps on a part-time basis, which can suit the employer well. Working from ten till three gives good cover to the lunch-hour, which can be busy at a time when full-time staff are having their own break.

On recruiting generally, Jim Moffat can almost define a profile of the person who will succeed at A.T. MAYS. The boy or girl will tend to be the 17-year-old who managed two Highers at school but didn't quite make it to university. They feel a sense of frustration, perhaps even failure, but suddenly they sense that here is a career at which they could succeed and, in the process, prove to their parents that the academic yardstick is not everything. Jim Moffat is in no doubt that that type of youngster makes the best recruit to the travel trade.

"They have this extra determination to do well," he says, "and they end up by doing better than if they had tried to be bankers or stockbrokers or whatever, if not financially at least with satisfaction in what they are doing.

"By the age of twenty-two, you will find that many of our young people have been to America, Hong Kong or Bermuda. They will have been dined and wined at the Hilton Hotel by tour operators and airlines who are most generous hosts to the travel trade. Filling planes with people from our business is seen as part of the training process. For example, there were about a hundred members of the A.T.MAYS staff on a Canberra cruise last year and that serves a very useful purpose for the shipping company as well as ourselves. When a customer comes into the shop with thoughts about a cruise, it is an obvious advantage if the assistant can give a first-hand account of what it is like."

A proportion of the girls who seek jobs with A.T. MAYS see the travel business as a fairly glamorous place and regard it perhaps as an *entrée* to a further career as an air stewardess. This view helps to bring hundreds of applications every month, mainly from girls, and affords the agency the privilege of being selective. Salaries may not be as high as in some other professions but the travel industry has never been a highly paid one.

For those young entrants, it goes without saying that it helps to be intelligent, good at selling, to have an interest in people and, perhaps above all, to be capable of undertaking accurate and detailed work at reasonable speed. It is a fairly broad base of talents which is helped greatly if there is a breezy and out-going personality behind it.

Jim Moffat explains: "Customers coming into a travel agency have more or less made up their minds that they are going to do something this summer. So I believe the holiday should start when they are received by a welcoming assistant who is showing a keen interest in their particular trip. They are looking for someone who will help to build up their own anticipation. Many of our staff do indeed build up a rapport with the customers and it is not at all uncommon for people to come in when they return to say how they got on and even to bring in a box of chocolates, in gratitude for the help they received."

Equally, staff have to be prepared to deal with complaints as well as bouquets. It is not everyone who comes in with chocolates in mind! It can be difficult, for example, to recommend hotels in places like Spain, which can be excellent one year and not so good the next. That may be due to nothing more than a change of manager, even a change of chef. Where there are genuine complaints, the agent has little difficulty with the reliable tour operator. A strong case will usually bring some redress. The first step is to ask the customer to put the complaint in writing. Sometimes it can turn out to be as trivial as "The soup was cold" and there are blatant cases where people are merely trying to get their money back for very little reason. Jim Moffat remembers the four girls who went to Belgium on their first-ever foreign trip. They came in to complain that their package was supposed to include a three-course meal and that, within that agreement, "there wis nae soup"!

So it is Lindsay Grattan's job to train staff for all contingencies, on most of which he can speak from personal experience. Like most senior staff, he has particular memories of the football charters which began to develop in the late 1960s as a direct spin-off from Celtic's memorable victory over Inter Milan in the European Cup Final of 1967. That year of the Lisbon Lions sparked off a new fashion for following the team into Europe, as well as the Scottish team to the World Cup, and the results were liable to border on the farcical.

Lindsay Grattan can still come out in a cold sweat at some of the hair-raising memories, like the one where Rangers were playing in Milan and A.T. MAYS was running charter planes from Prestwick. From his job as manager at Irvine, he found himself helping to see the supporters on their way to Italy. By 4 a.m., bus loads had arrived at the airport, spilling out their customers, many of whom were already the worse of the wear. Some checked in, then disappeared and the particular skill of the travel folk was to find enough of them to fill a plane and see it on its way. The Caledonian aircraft supplied a kind of shuttle service but, with the occupants in various conditions of alcoholic disarray, the travelling conditions were inclined to deteriorate by the time the final flight was turned towards the continent.

Getting them there may have been one thing but getting them back was another. Even when they had finally been rounded up and despatched to Scotland, the troubles were far from over. Back at his desk in search of recovery, Lindsay recalls being summoned to the counter of the Irvine office to deal with a man who was demanding to see the manager. Whereas some of the football supporters had flights only, others spent the night in Milan and had accommodation included in their package. This particular gent had just arrived back at Prestwick and had come straight to register his complaint. What confronted Lindsay was a fellow in a raincoat, suddenly pulling its flaps apart to reveal a pair of Y-fronts but no trousers! He had lost them in Italy. More precisely, his accommodation had been of a fairly basic nature, in which four strangers were liable to be sharing one room. Well oiled from the night's celebrations, he had eventually found the way to his bedroom, thrown his trousers down at the bedside and gone out like a light. Another occupant presumably had taken the opportunity to avail himself of a spare pair of trousers, complete with money, leaving the poor Scot to travel home in his drawers!

Sometimes, of course, it was the travel trade itself, not averse to a bit of socialising, which provided the alcoholic anecdote. Again football had a part to play in it. Scotland was playing in the World Cup in West Germany when Caledonian made a last-minute call to say they had found a spare aircraft and could fly out travel people who wanted to see Scotland's match. A.T. MAYS employees took up their quota of seats on the BAC 1-11 and not even the short notice prevented every one of them turning out in some sort of tartan display, from kilt to scarf or tammy. One of the travel agents on board played host with a bar and dispensed his offering in the rather unorthodox manner of coming down the aisle handing out a bottle of whisky between every two people. No glasses, just bottles. Such a gesture went down well, as you can imagine, and the national enthusiasm was heightened by the tartan-clad stewardesses singing over the intercom and a piper marching up and down the aisle. Even as the plane came in to land at Frankfurt, he was still squeezing the pigskin to the tune of "Scotland the Brave".

Looking back over his career, from the joyous to the bizarre, Lindsay Grattan remembers that bleak start in a cellar at Kilmarnock and realises that the fates were doing more than setting him out on a successful career. A. T. MAYS had recruited two beginners for the Kilmarnock office that week. The other beginner was young Mary McConnell. Five years later, Lindsay and Mary were married and, apart from leaving to have her daughter Anne, now a teenager, Mary has worked for A.T. MAYS over the same 26-year span as her husband. She is back in the Kilmarnock office, where she started, now working part-time.

CHAPTER THIRTEEN

A Bill from the Massage Parlour!

FOR all the care in selecting and training staff, Jim Moffat has long realised that the sudden exposure to travel and a taste of high living, at the expense of tour companies and airlines, was proving a test of character for many of his young people. For some, it has provided the notion of a living standard beyond their own means – and A.T. MAYS has not escaped the consequences of such aspirations.

The business was not long established, in fact, when suspicion fell on the staff at Kilmarnock, over missing money. They were summoned to headquarters in Saltcoats for a Perry Mason-type investigation and asked to account for themselves, one by one. As in all such incidents, the innocent were dragged in with the guilty, a fact well remembered by one of today's top managers. Fortunately, the culprit eventually confessed that he had been forging signatures. He turned out to be the manager, no less! For the sake of avoiding the publicity of prosecution, Jim Moffat decided not to press charges.

But people don't learn, not even from other people's mistakes. A girl in the Bellshill office finally explained that her occasional dips in the till were all to do with the fact that she was getting married and needed not only to buy a fur coat for herself but a car for her boyfriend!

The *pièce de resistance* of staff dishonesty, however, arose when bills began arriving for items not commonly available to A.T. MAYS employees. There was the white Rolls-Royce, complete with chauffeur, for example, engaged from London Airport to take a gentleman into the city. Then came a bill for the opulence of Claridge's Hotel, not to mention the services of Fifi, or some such obliging creature, at a massage parlour in Soho! The particular Walter Mitty character, who was living out his life of fantasy at other people's expense, had relieved the company of £26,000 before he was finally tracked down. He turned out to be a rather insignificant member of the head office staff, committed to a religious sect, as Jim Moffat recalls. He would make out cheques to a particular name and open an account in that name at a local bank, which was not as observant as it should have been in checking the identity of its new customer.

"I am not answerable to you," he apparently told Jim Moffat. "I have made my peace with the man upstairs." Tempted to have him by the throat, Mr Moffat was not inclined to leave the matter to the celestial courts and sought a more meaningful retribution on earth. After marking time as a guest of Her Majesty, the young man was brought before the court and ordered to give 200 hours of community service. Maybe the man upstairs had interceded after all.

Troubles did not come singly at that time. Having just installed the first computers at company headquarters, Jim Moffat found that someone had broken into the premises one night, jumped all over the computers and scattered the booking chits. "The staff arrived next morning to a heart-breaking sight," says the boss. "It threw us into total confusion about bookings and payments and, indeed, it very nearly put us out of business. We had lost half our records. The police were unable to pinpoint the culprit. I had my own idea who it was but had to keep my thoughts to myself!"

On a slightly lighter note, bundles of travellers' cheques stored in a basement of the Kilmarnock office became a temptation to a workman visiting the premises. He stole them all but, on the bus going home to Ayr, apparently took a scare and decided to dispose of them through the window. Consequently, there was a trail of A.T. MAYS' travellers' cheques fluttering all the way from Kilmarnock to Ayr that night!

That top manager of today who had to suffer investigation in that Kilmarnock fraud is none other than Dorothy Blane, who still remembers with horror the traumatic start to her career. Fortunately it did nothing to hamper her prospects and she stands today as manager of Bank Street, Kilmarnock, the number one branch in Scotland and one of the top three in the United Kingdom.

94

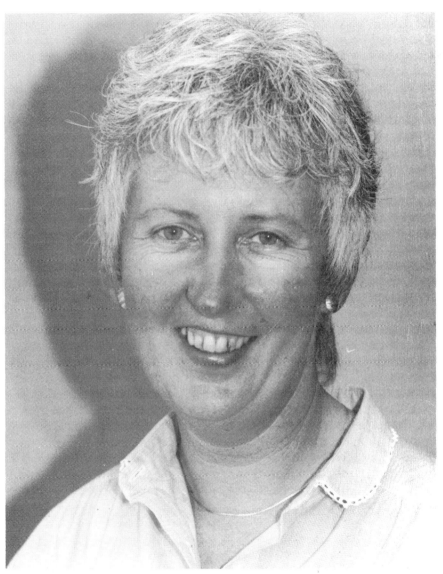

Mrs Dorothy Blane, Manager, Bank Street, Kilmarnock.

'TIS BETTER TO TRAVEL

Like Erl Macmillan, Dorothy's origins are in Fife, where her father was also a railwayman, like Erl, but he was transferred to Irvine and the family settled in Kilmarnock when Dorothy was eleven. Dux of her local school, she went to work for Saxone shoes before landing a job with A.T. MAYS. There was an early encounter with the boss. She had just been a week in the branch when Jim Moffat appeared one day. A customer was asking about a passport application and he said to Dorothy: "Can you deal with this?" As it happened, passports were all she had learned about so far and there was an early opportunity to impress the boss.

She moved to Saltcoats and then to the new branch at Irvine, which was first to operate charters. There was evidently much excitement as Dorothy, Janice and Mr Bromfield (father of Alan Bromfield, now deputy managing director), wrote out the tickets by hand and marshalled the customers on to coaches for Prestwick, en route to Canada by Aer Lingus. Dorothy returned to the Kilmarnock branch in Bank Street and has been there ever since, having spent 28 of her 44 years with the firm.

She had never been on an aeroplane when the chance came one day to join a Mercury Holiday flight for travel agents. It wouldn't seem much now but it was a novelty then to fly from Glasgow to Barcelona, take a walk round the terminal building and fly straight back to Glasgow! The horizons have broadened somewhat since then. Dorothy has seen Europe, Canada, the United States, Russia and Thailand and, more recently, has taken a party to Miami, en route to a Caribbean cruise. "When you have done it yourself, it is much easier to sell to the customer," she reaffirms.

Dorothy was married in 1965 but has no family and has therefore managed to run up an unbroken 28 years with the company. She became branch manager at Bank Street in 1976 and has observed changes over the years. How have the customers changed, for example?

"Compared to earlier days, the public are much clearer on where they want to go. They can tell you the foreign exchange rates and are generally better educated about travel. Not that that makes life any easier. In fact, I would say people are a little more awkward to deal with than they used to be. But I enjoy working with them and wouldn't like to lose the contact. Our branch is in a side street of Kilmarnock yet we produce some of the best figures in the company, including a lot of repeat business. Of the staff of 13, there are several with ten years' service or more and people get to know us personally."

How did staff react when they heard of the Royal Bank purchase?

A.T. MAYS conference get-together.

"When Mr Moffat phoned to tell us, I must say I found it a bit sad. We have always thought so much of him and were always treated as part of the family. But now we had grown so big and this had happened; I found myself thinking about those early days when there were only Saltcoats and Kilmarnock.

"Being under the Royal Bank hasn't changed things much. They don't bother with the everyday running of the business. A lot of our work nowadays is computerised but I sometimes think some of the younger staff concentrate too much on their screens instead of speaking to the customer."

Family stories abound within the framework of A.T. MAYS. Just as Jim Moffat had been a bank clerk with ambitions to be his own boss, so did Tom Killop of

97

Coatbridge begin to entertain similar thoughts. Tom was a riveter whose wife, Elizabeth, was one of those ladies who organised local bus runs. Every district has one. Tom had a streak of enterprise within him and concluded that there was money to be made from developing his wife's hobby. In 1956, he opened Killop's Travel Agency in Coatbridge and the whole family pitched in to make the venture a success. Son David was married that same year and he and his young wife, Colina, who worked in the local council offices, would come round to help out when they could. David worked with the British Steel Corporation.

Together, the family built a successful business, starting with the modest day-trip, through the local City Link bus depot, and spreading to sea crossings from Glasgow to Belfast and Dublin, providing a useful service for the large Irish connection in the Coatbridge population. The package tour followed in the normal manner and Killop's Travel Agency became well known in the Coatbridge area.

When Tom came towards retirement, however, his son was in a good position with British Steel and was reluctant to give it up. He and Colina did talk about taking it over but in the end it was decided to sell the business. That was how, in 1971, Killop's of Coatbridge became branch number 17 of A.T. MAYS, with Tom retained as a consultant, though he died within two years.

With a son then aged 12, Colina decided to go full-time and took on the job of assistant manager in the branch. Being taken over, she recalls, seemed a rather nerve-wracking experience but she looks back with satisfaction on how it all turned out. When she later accepted the manager's post at Coatbridge, she became the first woman to head a branch.

Meanwhile, David became redundant at British Steel and Jim Moffat was quick to bring him into the business, where he worked as cashier at Glasgow's Havelock Street and Duke Street. Then he was offered the manager's job at Alexandra Parade, Glasgow, a post he still holds, while his wife continued at Coatbridge. But the family connection doesn't end there. Their son Tom worked in travel for a time before moving on to British Steel, where his father had been. But his wife, Evelyn, who had been in the accounts department of Scotia Travel, was soon joining A.T. MAYS, where she did particularly well in the training course. Asked what she wanted to do in the firm, she opted for the business travel office at Royal Crescent, Glasgow, then became manager of the business house at East Kilbride. Finally she returned to Royal Crescent, where she led a staff of 23 while still in her twenties.

Looking back on her connection with A.T. MAYS, Colina Killop remembers amusing little incidents, like the day when a lady, ill accustomed to passports, was trying to answer the question about distinguishing marks. Her answer? Varicose veins!

Another elderly lady came in to say she didn't like the photograph in her passport and had decided to change it. She simply stuck on another, more flattering, one in its place, much against the law of course. They advised her to take it back to the passport office where "a very nice gentleman" told her she would have to start all over again, with a new passport.

Colina remembers, too, the case of the Coatbridge family emigrating to Australia and planning to take their dog with them. "We did everything to help them, including the information about injections required for the animal," she says. "We had the crate made and everything seemed to have gone fine. As they headed for their departure, we had a phone-call to say the dog was being sent back for three months because the vet had given it the wrong injections.

"You do become involved in people's arrangements and I nearly ended up by keeping the dog myself for the three months. In view of the mistake, however, the vet in question had to pay for the kennels during that period."

David and Colina Killop therefore represent the successful merging of one travel family with another, taking advantage of an amicable arrangement to embark upon new careers for themselves and their family. Like most other established employees, they have been everywhere from Canada, the Bahamas and Algiers to Florida, Texas and Turkey.

CHAPTER FOURTEEN

The Mystery Lady

GROOMED for a top job at A.T. MAYS, Alan Bromfield set out from Saltcoats to London on a September day of 1979 for what was to be an extended business trip to the United States. Uppermost in his mind was the fact that he would be travelling to Washington by Concorde, the first time he had ever been in that remarkable aeroplane.

Duly boarding at Heathrow, he found himself sitting alongside the only empty seat on the plane. So the eligible bachelor settled down, relishing the prospect of having the double space to himself, all the way to Washington. (He might also collect a double ration of the Concorde goody-bag.) Five minutes before take-off, there was still no occupant and his privacy seemed assured when the stewardess came to tell him there was good news and bad news. The bad news was that he was losing his empty seat; but the good news was that he would be joined by a lady. Ah well, life could be worse, thought bachelor Alan.

The lady in question had bustled up at the last minute, as was her wont, excused herself as she squeezed over to the window seat and settled down without any recognition from Alan, who was too much of a gentleman to study her at close quarters. He was immediately aware that she had travelled on Concorde before, judging by the familiarity with which she removed the head-rest and put it at her feet. She had a large, floppy handbag with papers falling out and seemed to be

Alan Bromfield, Deputy Managing Director.

in some state of disarray. Calling for a glass of iced water, with which she popped a pill, she rather opened the way for some side-long conversation with her Scots neighbour.

Though not perhaps as astute in star-spotting as might have been expected from a carefree bachelor, the intrepid Mr Bromfield nevertheless engaged the lady in small talk, noticed the name "Warner" on a piece of luggage and realised that she was who he should have known she was all along. At various stages of her life, of course, the name on the luggage could have been Fisher, Hilton, Wilding, Todd or Burton, as well as Warner, but the constant factor was that she was Elizabeth Taylor.

By now, some fellow travel agents on board, already ahead in the recognition stakes, were nudging him from all sides to convey their envy of his seat number. Meanwhile, the glamorous Miss Taylor was fuelling their envy by asking his name.

"I'm Alan Bromfield," he said.

"And I'm Elizabeth," she added superfluously.

"Yes, I had realised that," he said. And from then onwards the two were on first-name terms. They chatted for the entire three-and-a-half hours from London to Washington, except for 20 minutes – when the Hollywood star slept with her head on Alan's shoulder! You can imagine the banter. Between times, she entertained him with amusing tales of her husbands, from Michael Wilding to Mike Todd and Richard Burton.

She had clearly taken a shine to the man from A.T. MAYS – and had taken a shine to the Concorde silverware as well. So much so that she explained to the stewardess that she was collecting items for her daughter and would she please wrap up a set of Concorde silverware; oh, and while she was at it, bring one for her friend Alan too.

Meanwhile, Ian Stephen, a travel agent from the North-east, was pretending to be Lord Aberdeen in an attempt to introduce himself to the star.

"He's not really Lord Aberdeen, is he?" she inquired of Alan. By the time they reached Washington, Miss Taylor was calling for champagne before she was whisked away, whispering that this was the advantage of being a senator's wife. But, lo and behold, she was still there when he eventually came through Customs, calling him over to be introduced to her husband of the moment, Senator John Warner. She gave him a secretary's name to facilitate his entry to the Senate and, with a farewell kiss, was off, leaving one bewildered man from A.T. MAYS to be the envy of his fellow travellers.

Liz Taylor.

THE MYSTERY LADY

Clearly his bachelor's instincts were jogged out of their rut because Alan Bromfield went back to America some time later and married Jan, who was his cousin's
daughter. She was a widow with two children, who came to settle in Scotland,
with a home in Symington – an understanding lady who is very happy to turn out
that Concorde silverware in the knowledge that she landed the man who, for the
duration of a Concorde journey across the Atlantic at least, switched on the
glamorous film star who had been the subject of many a man's uncovered dreams.

Born in Glasgow in 1940, Alan Bromfield lived in Newton Mearns until the
family moved to Prestwick in 1947, when he went to Heathfield School and then
Ayr Academy. When he left in 1956, he began as a clerk with British Railways
at Drybridge, later serving at the district superintendent's office in Ayr before
deciding his future didn't lie with the railways.

Nevertheless, it was a background which lent itself, as in the case of many
others, to a career in the travel industry. By chance, his father had joined A.T.
MAYS in 1958, in the days of the wooden hut in Manse Street, and it seemed
like a good place to work so, in 1959, Alan Bromfield arranged an interview with
Jim Moffat. He still recalls the occasion with a mixture of surprise and merriment.
Finding his way along from Saltcoats Station to the ALL PETS shop, he made
his way inside and asked for Mr Moffat.

"There was this gent in the corner, in brown overalls, lifting seed from one con-
tainer to another. He turned and announced that he was Mr Moffat," Alan
remembers. "He dusted himself down and invited me round to the new premises
in Hamilton Street. There we went upstairs and I was perched on a box of Trill
while Mr Moffat sat himself down on the edge of another box. He then proceeded
to interview me while, at the same time, trimming the toe nails of a budgie! I had
never been to an interview before but not in my wildest imagination did I think
it would be like this. However, we both survived the experience, he decided to
employ me and I started in Bank Street, Kilmarnock, in 1959.

"There was a good family atmosphere, with a sense of cameraderie there, but
I have to say that we were working in fairly Dickensian conditions. I was down
in a basement, without windows, which is now a storage room."

In taking over the Mays branch in Kilmarnock, Jim Moffat had gained a fully
licensed business so Kilmarnock was, for the time being, the headquarters of the
company before being transferred to the home base of Saltcoats.

In interviewing the lad between the trimming of toe nails, Jim Moffat could
hardly have envisaged that he was engaging his future general manager and deputy

managing director. But that was the course upon which Alan Bromfield was set as he moved first to Largs to become branch manager at the age of 21, when the company bought over the Nugent business.

Settling into the only kind of digs he could afford in those days ("Pretty basic and a bit reminiscent of those digs in Ealing Studio comedies"), he was also beginning to realise one particular factor which dawns on many people in travel when they begin to settle in their new career: once you are in it, the job becomes something of an obsession, from which it is difficult to part company. For a start, travel was a great novelty 30 years ago and any youngsters entering the business were liable, as we have already learned, to find themselves *en route* to destinations which might seem modest enough today but were exciting adventures at the time. So the perquisites began to reveal themselves. Like most of his age-group, Alan Bromfield had never been on an aeroplane until he went on that trip from Prestwick to London and on to Belgium. The fact that there was a technical fault and a delay of eleven hours didn't seem to matter. Returning from London in 1960, he had his first experience of a jet-plane, a DC-8, which reached Prestwick in 50 minutes.

So Alan Bromfield cut his managerial teeth at Largs, with just one assistant, Ruth Williamson, and then jumped at the chance of moving to the new branch in Troon, which was convenient for his home in Prestwick as well as being counted fairly up-market in the developing business of A.T. MAYS. As a well-heeled little town, popular with retired people, it provided some of the aspects of travel not commonly encountered in the business, like customers wanting to winter in South Africa.

Jim Moffat had bought over the business and retained as a consultant the daughter of the original owner, Nessie Brown, with whom Alan remembers developing a kind of love-hate relationship. He remained at Troon until 1969 and it was during that period that the charter flight came into being in a big way. They were originally known as "ethnic flights" but later re-named "affinity charters", which meant, in theory, that the people had to be travelling in groups, belonging to the same club perhaps, or Cooperative Society, in order to gain the benefit of discount flights. That was the theory at least, though it was no secret that people found ways and means of attaching themselves to groups with which they had no affinity at all but which gave them access to the cheaper fare. Alan Bromfield remembers with some amusement the charter for members of the St Paul's Social Club from Hurlford, Kilmarnock, a Catholic organisation which raised a few eyebrows by the size of its in-flight demand for kosher food!

With the company expanding year by year, Alan's next interview with Mr Moffat was for the purpose of asking if he would like to move to head office in Saltcoats to become the boss's own personal assistant. As a means of broadening a young man's career, it was not an opportunity to be missed and Alan Bromfield jumped at it, at first retaining his links with the charter business until he handed that over to Lindsay Grattan, who later became personnel director. In his new role, Alan more or less shadowed Jim Moffat in his day-to-day business, becoming involved in discussions with the airlines and tour operators, who were beginning to sit up and take notice of this small-town travel company with an eccentric location on the Ayrshire coast of Scotland. Expansion was on its way and there was business to be done, no matter what the location.

The charter business was developing a new dimension with the arrival of Celtic Football Club on the European front and the willingness of football supporters to travel long distances to follow their team. The success of Celtic in defeating Inter Milan in the European Cup Final of 1967 had opened up new horizons and Alan Bromfield remembers being involved in the Glasgow club's second attempt to win that same cup, in Milan in 1970. Celtic were favourites to beat Feyenoord of Rotterdam and everybody, it seemed, wanted to be there for the big occasion. A.T. MAYS were offering the full range of opportunities, from a day-return to a seven-day excursion.

The midnight oil was being burned in the travel offices as staff tried to cope with the rush and the A.T. MAYS people worked throughout the night before Alan Bromfield was due to fly out to Milan in time to receive the first arrivals. Jim and Margie Moffat were in the office to set an example to the others but it was fairly noticable that Alan was reaching a stage of overwork where he looked punch-drunk through lack of sleep.

It was one of those occasions well suited to the impish humour of Jim Moffat, who was sure he had the answer to Alan's exhaustion. To tide him over, he produced a pep-pill which turned out to be none other than a Bob Martin dog powder! It was one of the more bizarre examples of how convenient it could be to run a pet shop and a travel shop at the same time. Whatever the veterinary ingredients, Bob Martin kept Alan Bromfield awake, bright-eyed and bushy-tailed, until he reached Milan and started the mammoth task of receiving the hordes of high-spirited Scottish football fans. Though they were using an airport well outside of town, they succeeded in conveying them all to their various hotels around Milan and arranging to have them taken to the stadium for the big night.

'TIS BETTER TO TRAVEL

The fact that the day-excursion supporters were due to gather again in the city square to meet the bus for a midnight departure was, in retrospect, an ambitious arrangement, especially when Celtic unexpectedly lost and there was an abundance of sorrows to be drowned. (Conversely, of course, it would have been over-ambitious even if they had won, when there would have been much celebrating in mind.) Anyway, when departure time for the first coach arrived, there were no more than a dozen of the first plane-load on hand to board it, representing the sober element of a highly charged night. Alan Bromfield had managed to snatch some sleep in the afternoon and was up in good time to cope with the ensuing chaos. As the planes were delayed, pilots were running out of flying hours, which further complicated the schedules. All Alan remembers is that it took 48 hours to clear the muddle, a highly-profitable exercise for people like A.T. MAYS but one which he reckons added a few forehead furrows and lost him two stones in weight from anxiety and lack of sleep.

Vowing that he would not like to go through that experience again, he soon found that anything the Celtic supporters were capable of doing, the Rangers' following could more than match. Within two years he was on the European trail again, this time to see that A.T. MAYS' portion of the 20,000 Rangers supporters would reach Barcelona in time to see the European Cup Winners' Cup Final with Moscow Dinamo. This time there was victory for the Scots, with consequences which proved that the travel agent was bound to suffer either way. It is well on record that the Rangers' supporters did a fair imitation of tearing Barcelona apart that night. All the experience of Milan had not prepared Alan Bromfield for the battles of Barcelona. Apart from the chaos at the airport, he discovered that two of his "guests" in a Barcelona hotel had been fighting on a balcony, with the result that one fell over and had to be removed to hospital. The man on the balcony was soon incarcerated in the town jail. Of course, nobody had been drinking, according to themselves. Perhaps they were just too stoned to know! Along in another hotel – the one where George Sanders died, they said – there was another group making a pretty realistic attempt at setting the lift on fire.

But even when the pilgrims had been safely delivered back to Scotland, the troubles were not over. Just as, on a previous excursion, that chap had arrived back without his trousers, there were two deliriously happy Rangers' supporters on an A.T. MAYS' charter who were already back at Glasgow Airport – and looking for their car in the car-park – before they were struck by a disturbing flash of recollection. In the euphoria of champagne celebrations, they forgot that they

108

Rangers supporters en route *to Barcelona.*

had driven across Europe to the match – AND THEIR CAR WAS STILL IN BARCELONA!

Throughout the 1970s, there were many more excursions by bus and plane to football internationals at Wembley but eventually the hooligan element made it all too difficult, in the manner we have come to know, and spoiled what could have been great fun for them – and good business for the travel trade.

Having gained valuable experience as personal assistant to the chairman, Alan Bromfield became general manager of the company and was much involved with Thistle Air, which had been an air-broking company. In 1971, the rules governing those affinity tours were changed and A.T. MAYS became the joint owners of Thistle Air along with the inimitable Freddie Laker, through his Laker Airways. Thistle became the general sales agents for Laker Airways but that is a story in itself.

Meanwhile, Alan Bromfield had been made a director of the company in 1979 and deputy managing director in 1987.

CHAPTER FIFTEEN

Freddie Laker Flies In

ONE morning in February of 1982, a Laker Airways plane was approaching Gatwick on a flight from Rome when the pilot came on the public address system. He had given his passengers time to digest their breakfast before breaking the news which was already going down with the cornflakes all over the country: Freddie Laker, the colourful cavalier of British flying, had gone bust.

Everyone was deeply upset because Laker had become something of a folk-hero, the rugged Londoner who took on the airline giants and engaged them in a battle which brought down fares and opened up the possibility of transatlantic travel to countless thousands who could not have contemplated it otherwise. On an historic day of 1977, 272 passengers had taken off for America at a cost of just £59 each.

The sadness at Laker's demise was felt by no one more strongly than Jim Moffat, whose concern for the man was compounded by the fact that he was also his partner in business. Looking ahead as ever, Jim had observed the trend of the charter business in the 1960s and decided that he could do much worse than to align himself with an airline. The man whose name was on everyone's lips at that time was Freddie Laker, a kind of swashbuckling character who gained his first working capital from a successful deal in Government surplus trucks after the war. Then, it is said, with a loan of £38,000 from a man in a pub, he bought six

Freddie Laker.

converted Halifax bombers which he flew in the notorious Berlin Airlift of 1948. From then it was a steady progress into the independent airline business, catching the public imagination with his attempts to bring them lower fares.

Who better to approach, thought Mr Moffat, than Mr Laker himself? It was the start of a business relationship, even friendship, which Jim Moffat recalls with warmth, amusement and even some amazement to this day. Laker suggested to Moffat that, as a first step towards entering the bigger league of chartering, he should link up with someone in what was known as the Baltic Exchange – the people involved in shipping and air-broking. There was a company called Kendall

112

within that membership and, in a three-way partnership, Jim Moffat found himself forming the company called Thistle Air Brokers Ltd, in which he held a 50 per cent share, with Freddie Laker owning 26 per cent and Kendall 24 per cent. This was the vehicle required to give him access to quotations for aircraft as and when required.

Kendall were soon to be taken over by Tiny Rowland's Lonrho company but before this actually took place Jim Mofatt stepped in and bought out their share of Thistle, becoming a 74 per cent shareholder, alongisde Laker's 26 per cent. They were battling along reasonably well when, suddenly, Laker branched into his much-publicised Skytrain venture, a walk-on, walk-off, no-frills service at a cost which no one had thought was possible. It operated from Prestwick to New York and, in Thistle Air, he had a ready-made agent in Scotland, able to look after ticket sales as well as general handling arrangements for the Skytrain flights. Moffat and Laker were now in big business together, a connection which intrigued the flying Cockney all the more when he discovered that he and Jim Moffat's wife, Margie, were born on exactly the same day – 8 August 1922. He was equally intrigued by the prospects of what they were building up together, with flights rising into the western sky from Prestwick en route to places like New York, Miami and Vancouver.

Like most courageous people who venture into the airline business, Laker was always walking on a tightrope which could have you on the heights one day and possibly on a free-fall the next. It had happened before and it has happened since. But the public have a sneaking regard for entrepreneurs of that sort, knowing that they themselves are likely to be the beneficiaries if all goes well – and wishing them good luck in their competition against the Goliaths of the sky. He was almost Mrs Thatcher's model of the enterprise culture and received much encouragment from her. He had also, by then, received a knighthood.

"I look back on Freddie Laker as a good guy, a man of tremendous charisma," Jim Moffat later reflected. "But, like so many people who perhaps think they can walk on water as well as fly over it, he found things were beginning to go against him. The pound went against him for a start. He was leasing aircraft on very high repayment terms and biting off more than he could chew. In addition, the big airlines were ganging up against him. There is no doubt about that."

Jim Moffat had been in partnership with Laker since 1967 until the big collapse came in 1982. His struggle to repay ambitious bank loans finally came unstuck. Public reaction was quite emotional. Just as he had the support of the public, there

113

Leslie Havlin, Manager of Thistle Air.

was a loyal staff around him, pitching in to help him survive and shedding copious tears when he finally had to admit defeat.

It was the battle of the individualist fighting the system and gaining the plaudits of the massed ranks on the terracing. In the world of fiction, such figures emerge as heroes. In reality, too often, they tend to disappear into the ranks of the defeated, proving what a battle it can be to survive in the ruthless arena of big-time business.

When Laker went out in honourable defeat, however, the gentle giant of the Scottish travel trade managed to rescue his Thistle Air part of Laker's enterprise, which managed to escape without financial damage. It still survives to this day, in a very big way as specialists in North American travel, owned one hundred per cent by A.T. MAYS and adding its six-figure profits to the overall total profits of around £2.5 million.

Jim Moffat still remembers visiting Freddie Laker in his office at Gatwick Airport. It was up several floors in an old hangar, without a lift and presenting a testing climb. When he was chosen Businessman of the Year, he took Jim and Margie Moffat to lunch at the Copthorne Hotel in Gatwick, jocularly brushing aside the dignified waiter who was offering an expensive wine and saying, with a thriftiness which would commend itself to his Scottish guests, that he would have the cheaper house wine instead. To prove, however, that money was no object, at that point at least, the Moffats were entertained aboard the Laker yacht at Cannes.

On one of his inaugural flights from Prestwick, the guests included the famous Ma Broon from Paisley, who organised so many of the A.T. MAYS club flights under the "Paisley Buddies" banner. Laker knew her value as a drummer-up of business for those charter flights to America and made a great fuss of her. Jim Moffat later asked her what she had thought of Mr Laker. In characteristically down-to-earth tones, she passed her own verdict: "Ach, he's just a big chancer!"

At the sharp-end of that A.T. MAYS connection with Sir Freddie was a former Burns and Laird shipping clerk, Leslie Havlin, who had become manager of Thistle Air. He remembers the experience like this: "When Laker started, we were handling just about everything for him. He ran from Prestwick, Manchester and London in those days and we used to get together and work out what flights were needed, on what days and so on, for the following year. It was all put into a brochure and Freddie Laker would put a truck on the road to Scotland, where we would be his distributors. I remember being up to the neck in brochures. We went round the travel agents to dish out his stock. But that was just the start of it. We did the reservations and confirmations, we wrote the tickets and, in fact, did everything for Laker in Scotland. At that stage, in 1973, his routes from Scotland went from Prestwick to Toronto but, by the end of the 1970s, the programme had expanded to take in New York, Detroit, Miami and Los Angeles. We were flying from Prestwick to all those destinations and, in the early 1980s, we had started inclusive packages to Miami. In fact, we were just promoting that particular package when he went bust. That was a traumatic experience, as you can imagine. Laker was 99 per cent of Thistle Air's business and building up all the time so, being as heavily involved as that, we wondered where we could go from there.

"During the previous winter, as it happened, we had started talking to North West Airlines about their programme across the Atlantic and had reached agreement about the sale of their products. When the Laker collapse came, we had to transfer quickly our business to North West. It is not hard to see that 1982 would scarcely be regarded as a good year. In clearing up the mess, we had to find alternative arrangements for the people who had booked with Laker Airways. It was not an easy time but, from 1982 onwards, we have been expanding our programme with North West and that has gone well for us.

"Yet, looking back on Freddie Laker, I can remember him only as a very personable and approachable man, one of those people who always managed to remember your name, no matter how seldom you saw him. He was a great frontman for an airline and, indeed, if anyone else had been in that position, the venture would not have done so well as it did. He caught the public imagination and they responded in the way that people do to someone who is trying to give them a better deal. He deserved to succeed and it was a great pity that he didn't last."

For Leslie Havlin, it was a highlight in an interesting career which he had started locally, on that ferry service which Burns and Laird ran from Ardrossan to Belfast. For two years, Leslie was dealing with freight and passengers across the Irish Sea before contacting A.T. MAYS to see if there were any jobs available.

Again, like former railway employees, shipping clerks were natural candidates for the travel trade, having been geared to the movement of people and bringing with them some sense of what the agency business was all about. Jim Moffat engaged Leslie Havlin in 1963 and sent him to work at the Hamilton Street branch in the home town of Saltcoats. He served there as a junior clerk before

Scottish European Airways H. S. 1 + 8 aircraft.

being sent as branch manager at Largs, following the example of Alan Bromfield, and proving once again that youth was no barrier to promotion. If you were good enough, you were old enough.

By now, A.T. MAYS was gaining momentum and the expansion of Jim Moffat was starting. Young Havlin was brought back to head office and, as other agencies were bought over, he was entrusted with the task of going out to spend three or four months with the staff, bringing them into the fold with his guidance on how the new owner wanted his business run.

In 1972, Leslie Havlin was made manager of Thistle Air, which had formerly been an air-broking company, now turning to its new purpose with the arrival of Advance Booking Charters, commonly known as ABC. The function of Thistle Air, then and now, differs from other aspects of A.T. MAYS' business in that Thistle operates at the wholesale level while the branches are the equivalent of retail shops. In other words, they undertake some of the functions for which retailers normally look to the bigger organisations, like Thomson Holidays and Intasun – putting together the packages for the travel agencies to sell over the counter.

Quite naturally, A.T. MAYS take up to 60 per cent of Thistle Air business but its services are available to their retail competitors, like Thomas Cook and Lunn Poly. The main thrust of the business is based on flight-only bookings but with the full service of holiday bookings, car-hire, rail and bus tickets available as required.

The research and contacts required for putting the various aspects together are clearly something which the travel agency, at the sharp end, would not have time to arrange. Thus the wholesale part of the trade and the vast range of countries are something with which Thistle Air must acquaint itself. It does business with every country from Canada, the United States, Australia and New Zealand to South Africa and the Far East. "We are expanding all the time," say Leslie Havlin, "and it becomes more and more the case that we can put together a package which will meet the customer's requirements precisely."

He and his staff of 12 are based in Kilmarnock, next door to the retail branch in Bank Street. Having stayed in the area virtually all his life, he is married to Joyce and they live in Stevenston, adjoining Saltcoats.

Since the Royal Bank deal had to be secured without advance publicity, Leslie was one of many employees to whom it came as something of a shock. He happened to be on holiday at the time, went in to buy a copy of the *Glasgow Herald* – and there it was on the front page. Like everyone else at A.T. MAYS, he has been a supporter of retaining Prestwick Airport. In pragmatic terms, they have all known that, if the worst comes to the worst, the operators will move to Glasgow and business will have to continue as usual.

CHAPTER SIXTEEN

The Premier Division

IN the public mind, there is frequent confusion about the relationship of travel agents and tour operators. By and large, they are separate entities, though there is some cross-fertilisation, as in the case of Lunn Poly, the agent, being owned by Thomson International, the operator.

To clarify the division, there are, on the one side, the travel agents, the Big Five of which are Thomas Cook, Pickford's, Lunn Poly, A.T. MAYS and Hogg Robinson. Their number of branches and market share of the package tours for 1987, with estimates for 1988, are roughly as follows:

	ABTA branches	Package Tours Market share	
		1987	1988 (Est.)
Lunn Poly	484	10.5%	15%
Pickford's	371	7.0%	8%
Thomas Cook	364	11.5%	10%
A.T. MAYS	264	3.5%	4.5%
Hogg Robinson	245	4.5%	4.0%
W.H. Smith	198	2.0%	3.5%

'TIS BETTER TO TRAVEL

The most noticeable factor, as mentioned elsewhere, is the explosive increase in the role of Lunn Poly, rising by more than 100 branches in one year and gaining an increase in tour business of around 50 per cent.

On the other side, the tour operators exist to put together the packages which those travel agents sell. These include companies like Intasun and Horizon while, on the smaller scale, you find companies like Falcon, Sol and Speedbird, which is 50 per cent owned by British Airways and specialises in up-market trips to distant places, like the Far East. Some small companies exist to provide a very specialised type of holiday, like ski-ing or safaris to Kenya.

By far the biggest player in the tour operating game, however, is Thomson Holidays, now the largest not just in Britain or Europe but the world, especially since its purchase of Horizon Holidays in 1988. Thomson is part of that empire which orginated with the remarkable Roy Thomson, a Canadian who came to Scotland quite late in life, during the 1950s, gained the franchise for Scottish Television and declared that to be "a licence to print money". He came with the benefit of vast experience of broadcasting stations in Canada and was well ahead of British thinking when he came here. His frankness was still surprising. Roy Thomson also acquired the *Scotsman* newspaper in Edinburgh and bought out the extensive empire of Lord Kemsley, whose newspaper chain stretched from the *Sunday Times* in London to the *Press and Journal* in Aberdeen. He became Lord Thomson of Fleet, a man who extended his business interests into everything from oilfields to the travel industry. With such foresight and vision, it is not all that surprising that his tour company was set to become the world's number one.

From the outside view, however, it might seem that Thomson's are in a rather invidious position when they own a large travel agency like Lunn Poly and also serve the rivals of their own company, like A.T. MAYS, who depend a great deal on the packages which Thomson puts together. It is not, however, a problem which bothers the regional sales boss, Mrs Nesta Christie, who runs the Scottish end of Thomson Holidays from her office at 78 Queen Street, Glasgow. Fair-mindedness apart, of course, the forces of market reality come into it. A company like A.T. MAYS is not there to be ignored or given second best, as Nesta Christie explains: "My relationship is that I work with all the travel agencies on an equal basis. We are here to serve all the Scottish trade and A.T. MAYS is extremely important to us because it is so dominant in Scotland. If Lunn-Poly and A.T. MAYS are both looking for brochures at the same time, they are treated in exactly the same way.

"Lunn Poly is certainly our biggest client on the national scale, with A.T. MAYS coming fourth, after Thomas Cook and Pickford. But on the Scottish scene, A.T. MAYS is the number one and therefore a highly significant part of our business."

How that business has expanded in the 1980s can be seen from the fact that, as boss of Thomson in Scotland and dealing with flights from Glasgow, Edinburgh and Aberdeen, Nesta Christie was reckoning with 30,000 people flying out from Glasgow in the early eighties and, by the end of that decade, the figure had gone up to more than 200,000 in summer bookings and 70,000 in winter. A.T. MAYS has obviously played a significant part in that expansion.

A native of Glasgow, Nesta Christie began her career in the travel business with Mackay Brothers before moving to Nairn Travel which, by coincidence, was later bought by A. T. MAYS, though after she had left. Nesta next moved to Sky Tours which was, in turn, bought by Thomson. With more than 20 years in the business, she has had time to assess the companies and the personalities involved. Travel people know a good deal about each other and she recalls having known the name of Jim Moffat from the very start of her career.

"In my dealings with A.T. MAYS," she says, "I have always felt very clearly that Mr Moffat was running the company. Any A.T. MAYS decision has a Jim Moffat feel about it. He is such a well respected figure in the trade and it is easy to see why.

"It is just a small incident but I remember going to the A.T. MAYS headquarters in Saltcoats one day and, from his window, he had seen me arriving in the car park. Apparently he didn't know I was coming but the next I knew he was out to greet me in the car park. Not too many people would bother to do that. So you come to think of him as a lovely gentleman.

"We see people at sales conferences and you always see Mr Moffat treating people well. He is always speaking to his staff, especially the long-serving ones. He obviously regards them as friends, almost as one of the family.

"When my English colleagues come to Scotland they are always amazed that there is still such courtesy and good manners around, that men will still stand up when a woman comes into the room. All that is embodied in Jim Moffat, who is the kind of man who will hold a door open for you. We women may want to be on equal terms with the men but it is nice to think you can have the equality without taking away that kind of courtesy.

"In your business dealings with a man like that, you try harder to make things

121

right, feeling that, if you don't, you may have disappointed not just a business colleague but a friend.''

Nesta Christie has that same respect for the whole Moffat family and feels that son Jamie, in following the tradition, is coming through as his own person and taking up the difficult challenge of following such a successful father.

CHAPTER SEVENTEEN

The Man Who Made Majorca

JIM MOFFAT made his appearance in the travel business at perhaps the most opportune moment the fates could have designed for him. There was just enough time to serve an apprenticeship before the modern boom in holiday traffic would break upon the British scene, at the beginning of that decade which became known as the Swinging Sixties.

With that mixture of business acumen and native shrewdness, the former bank clerk from Saltcoats was just the kind of man to progress in that burgeoning industry which would open up a whole host of opportunities for those with the entrepreneurial spirit. When you study the method of his expansion – using successive profits to finance the next move without incurring a crippling debt of borrowing – it is not hard to understand how he grew from that humble beginning in a wooden hut in Saltcoats to the fourth biggest travel agent in Britain, with nearly 300 branches.

Putting aside the good timing of his arrival, it is interesting to speculate what pattern of progress he might have followed if he had emerged, say, 50 years earlier, into a vastly different travel trade. Though the mass market in tourism was half a century away, there was nevertheless a thriving travel business in the earlier part of this century, albeit to do with a widespread emigration of people who would probably never come back to Scotland – and a wealthy clientèle who would go

The sign remains "Llewelyn Davies", now A.T. MAYS, Queen Street, Glasgow.

by train to the South of France or Switzerland or just as readily embark on a world cruise. The possible scenario for a man like Jim Moffat can perhaps best be gauged from what happened to another man of enterprising spirit, whose name became quite famous in Scotland. Indeed, the story of T. Llewelyn Davies symbolises much of what travel meant in the first half of the century and the stature of the man is all the more remarkable when you consider that, apart from a sub-office in Paris, he never had more than one point of business – a bustling office at 21 Queen Street, Glasgow, just off Argyle Street.

Everyone knew the name of Llewelyn Davies, the Welshman from Denbigh, who went to work for Thomas Cook in London before being sent north to open up a banking and exchange department in their Glasgow office in 1899. By 1913, he had decided to shed the mantle of employee and, not unlike Jim Moffat, to branch out on his own, acquiring his premises in Queen Street, opening up as a currency dealer at first and acting as the Glasgow banker for Samuel Montague of London among other things. Already well known in his adopted city, he gained such a high reputation in his new business that he soon became the centre of currency activity in Glasgow, the man with whom even the big banks did their exchange. Every Friday, the managers of the main banks went round to Queen Street to transact their business.

Llewelyn Davies was eventually joined in the business by his two sons, Llewelyn and Lloyd, who pursued separate careers before returning to Queen Street and emerging as significant figures in their own right. Llewelyn junior used his London banking experience to look after the currency side while brother Lloyd concentrated on the travel, gaining his own share of fame as the man who "discovered" Majorca in the 1930s and started the great trek which has turned that Balearic island into the most popular holiday resort the Scots have ever known.

Happily, Lloyd Davies is still with us, a jolly little man who lives on the south edge of Glasgow with a fund of memories about travel before the Second World War, and who still ventures off to Puerto Pollensa two or three times a year, where he is fêted as the man who put that town on the map as a summer resort.

When the original Llewelyn Davies came north to Glasgow, he met and married Catherine Walker, whose father built a large part of Troon, before settling to his business in Queen Street. The trade was vastly different in 1913. For a start, there was only a handful of travel shops in Glasgow, his rivals being confined to Moses Buchanan of Renfield Street, Pitt and Scott of Dixon Street, and his former

125

employers, Thomas Cook of Buchanan Street, with whom he was in fairly high-powered competition.

Career patterns were much less conventional in those far-off days, as witness the case of one Robert Gibson, who left Thomas Cook to join Llewelyn Davies in Queen Street and later pursued his religious interests to Rome, where he ended up as an interpreter at the Vatican!

Llewelyn Davies junior, born in 1903, rejoined his father from London banking in 1926 and Lloyd Davies, born in 1908, started his career with Arthur and Company, the well-known warehouseman in the centre of Glasgow, before joining the Anchor Line as a purser.

It is difficult for the generation in the latter part of the 20th century to visualise that Glasgow scene between the wars, when there was not only a hive of industry surrounding the dockside area of the River Clyde but a massive employment in heavy engineering. How could you explain to a youngster today such a regular spectacle as a railway locomotive being transported down the centre of High Street from its cradle at Springburn, en route to the mighty crane at Finnieston, which would load it on board a ship with a destination which could be anywhere in the world?

Apart from the sheer volume of shipbuilding, producing some of the greatest liners the world has ever seen, imagine the drama of those floating hotels setting out every Friday night from Yorkhill Quay to the distant romance of New York. What a spectacle for young and old alike to gather at the quayside as those ships hooted their goodbyes in the evening mist, not to mention the equal excitement of the inward sailings, bringing celebrities and adventurers from faraway places. Out from the heart of Glasgow went those ships of the Anchor Line, Canadian Pacific and Anchor-Donaldson, heading for North America and beyond, with famous names like the *California*, *Cameronia*, *Transylvania* and *Athenia*, up to 2,000 passengers on board.

In his role as purser, Lloyd Davies still recounts great tales of sailing away on those voyages, calling only at Moville, in Northern Ireland, to collect more emigrants who had gathered from all over the Emerald Isle. As they boarded the ship for a new life in Ameica, they took their farewells of loved ones on the quayside and many a lump was raised in the throat as the tearful partings were sealed with a communal rendering of the "Londonderry Air".

Lloyd Davies, who left the Anchor Line to join his father in 1931, had already the experience of a world cruise behind him when he embarked on what was one of the highlights of his career. With the Empire Exhibition at Bellahouston Park, Glasgow, in 1938, Scotland had just witnessed its biggest ever event, attracting more than 13 million people from all over the world. In the following year, the massive New York World Fair was due to attract the same international audience and many a Scot was anxious to cross the Atlantic for the spectacular event. T. Lleweleyn Davies decided to organise a special cruise to New York and teamed up with the Anchor Line to use the *California* and re-title it for the occasion as "Scotland's Ship of Friendship". Under the guidance of Lloyd Davies, hundreds filed on board that July day of 1939 to sail away in high spirits on a voyage which was heartily endorsed by Lord Provost Patrick Dollan, who commended the educational value of travel and reminded them all that the World Fair in New York, like the Empire Exhibition in Glasgow, had been planned for peace, friend-ship and democracy.

For as little as £27.5s per head, the Scots set out on the adventure of a lifetime, a harmony ruffled a little by a dispute about who would hand over a silver salver to the famous Mayor of New York, Fiorella Henry La Guardia, who later gave his name to the airport outside the city. The contestants were some of Glasgow's Labour town councillors, who thought they should be given the honour, and Sir John Henderson, the bowler-hatted Tory MP for Cathcart, who was also in the party. Lloyd Davies mediated and it was agreed that Sir John should bear the salver towards the mayor – an honour which cost him not a little when the Customs men demanded that, mayor or no mayor, the gift would cost its bearer a cool 20 dollars! However, the Scots toured the sights of New York, took in the World Fair, went up to Boston and sailed for home.

Those noble words about peace, friendship and democracy reverberated uneasily that night, in August of 1939, when the lights of the *California* went sud-denly dead and those passengers heading home to Glasgow realised that the rumblings of war were not far off and that they were experiencing the very first of what would become known as the Black-out.

Lloyd Davies hastened home to a world which was, nevertheless, not yet at war and was trying to maintain all signs of normality. With merchant shipping still sailing freely on the high seas, he was being asked to book passages to Canada and the United States, sometimes by people who were thinking of taking their children away from the threatened dangers. At the office in Queen Street, they had booked many people on board the passenger liner *Athenia*, which was due to sail the Atlantic at the beginning of September. On the very day war was declared,

127

the *Athenia* was already heading out into the ocean when along came a German U-boat with the torpedo which sank the great old ship, at a cost of 112 lives, some of them women and children – and many of them the customers of the Llewelyn Davies family in Queen Street. The *Athenia* goes into the history books, therefore, as the first ship to be sunk in the Second World War. Alas, in the great catalogue of naval tragedies during the war, it was to be followed by so many other names well known to Glaswegians, including the *Transylvania* and the same *California* which took those carefree Scots to the World Fair in New York.

At the beginning of that war, Llewelyn Davies junior went off to serve in the Marines while Lloyd joined the RAF, only to be invalided out an early stage. Then came another chance to serve at sea. Over coffee at Lang's Restaurant one day, an old friend, Ian Bruce, told him they needed a purser on the *Britannia*, a ship Lloyd Davies knew well from his days of taking parties on cruises. He knew Captain Collie and he knew David Purdie from Shawlands, Glasgow, who was also serving on the ship. He was sorely tempted. But his father, the original Llewelyn Davies, was entering his final months and the family lawyer advised against it.

The *Britannia* sailed without Lloyd Davies and was just off Portugal when she was sunk by a German battleship. His friends, Ian Bruce and Captain Collie, were both lost. A lifeboat with 78 people drifted across the Atlantic but when it reached South America there were only 15 survivors. The lad he knew from boyhood, David Purdie, was one of them.

Back home, Lloyd Davies was performing a task which would seem strangely alien to a travel agent today. With millions of Jews fleeing the Nazi tyranny in Europe, the Jewish Refugee Committee in Scotland enlisted the aid of Lloyd Davies to help them find new destinations abroad. He would travel to London to seek a pass from Scotland Yard which would allow him to visit refugee camps in Britain. There he would obtain lists of names and bring them back for vetting, in case there were hidden Nazis in the ranks. Thereafter, he set about finding them passages to countries like the United States, a vastly different exercise from his pre-war days of guiding the affluent to their continental resorts.

It was a liaison which brought the Davies family a tremendous amount of good-will from the Jewish community and a great deal of private business thereafter, not that it was possible to do much travelling in those bleak, post-war years when restrictions were everywhere, food rationing was still in force, the austerity of Sir Stafford Cripps, the Chancellor of the Exchequer, was legendary – and foreign travel had a limit of £25 spending money.

128

THE MAN WHO MADE MAJORCA

Air France did manage to institute a service from Prestwick to Paris and Llewelyn Davies were major customers, with Lloyd Davies paying weekly visits to the French capital and establishing a small office in Rue d'Alger. Gradually life was restored to the travel business, with customers managing to find their way back to some of the top Mediterranean resorts like Nice. There were other names to add to the travel agents of the early days, like Donald Mackenzie Travel and Mackay of Bath Street, as well as Williamson's of Hope Street, which became the American Express.

Once Britain had shaken off the yoke of war, there would be a new desire for relaxation and perhaps a taste of foreign travel in those who had served overseas and found new horizons. They may still want Millport but they might just as easily seek Magaluf. Lloyd Davies was already planning ways to resume an ambitious plan which had been cut short by the war and dated back to that world cruise he undertook as a junior purser with the Anchor Line in 1928. The cruise included a stop at the beautiful Balearic island of Majorca which was then, believe it or not, a winter resort only, frequented by the upper classes of Europe, many of them escaping the rigours of the northern freeze-up. It occurred to young Lloyd Davies that there was a much greater potential than this and he stored away the thought until he joined his father's business three years later.

It was then that he noticed a feature of the Paddy Henderson shipping line, which ran a passenger service from Liverpool to Rangoon. People coming home on holiday to Britain from the Far East would disembark at Marseilles, catch the quicker train through France, to gain extra days at home – and do the same on the way back. Henderson's ships therefore had lots of empty berths between Merseyside and the Mediterranean. That gave Lloyd Davies the idea of striking a deal with Paddy Henderson about taking up the slack at very attractive prices. He would take the customers to Liverpool by train and onward to Majorca in Paddy Henderson's empty berths.

When it all began in 1934, he was largely restricted to the traditional winter holidays but gradually he persuaded the Majorcans that there was much business to be done in the summer. Among his early contacts in Majorca was a certain Herr Strohmeyer, a hotelier with an uncommon number of German waiters. It was much later he discovered they were trainees in a secret U-boat base and that *der Herr* was up to much more than hotel-keeping. For all he knew, they were probably the people who helped to sink the *Athenia* and other well-known ships from Glasgow. Trying to build up that business in the 1930s, Lloyd Davies was there just days before the outbreak of the Spanish Civil War which, in turn, ran into the Second World War; so it was more than 12 years before he could plan to resume the connection. Even then, in the early 1950s, it took six-and-a-half hours of a plane-changing marathon to get from Prestwick to Paris and Barcelona and finally to Palma.

In those early days, places like Palma Nova didn't exist beyond a stretch of sand and a little hut selling lemonade. Nowadays there are colonies of hotels, which can give rise to some cynical comments about Blackpool with sunshine. By then, however, Lloyd Davies was trying to pioneer the development of a corner of Majorca which was closest to his heart, Puerto Pollensa, which remains one of the more desirable parts of the island today. It was a vastly different place when he first drove in. For all its potential, there were only two hotels in the whole place, the Sis Pins and Illa d'Or, and there was a drastic sewage problem in this old Roman town, with an aroma which was guaranteed to send you elsewhere.

Lloyd Davies took an interest in their problems, became involved with the local people and was co-opted to a local tourist board, advising them on means of overcoming the sewage hazard, including a tax on those who would benefit from a holiday influx as a source of finance. Pollensa thus became the delightful resort it is today and Lloyd Davies of Scotland became something of a local hero, decorated by the Spanish Tourist Board for his services to their major industry. He and his wife Jean are invited to christenings, weddings and funerals as if they were members of the family. One of their great friends is the lad who was bell-boy at their hotel in those early days. Miguel Pericas now owns two hotels in the town, the Capri and Pollentia, and the two families play host to each other on their visits to Scotland and Majorca.

So this remarkable Scot who virtually put Majorca on the summer holiday map was in a privileged position when the business did begin to pick up in the late 1950s, by which time he was joined in competition with other firms, such as A.T. MAYS. Though they were in line for the start of the big boom, the Davies brothers had already reached an age when it would have been foolhardy to contemplate expansion. Without being too élitist, they had lived through a vastly different age, as can be seen from the preceding story. Of course they conveyed the emigrants on their one-way trips to the New World but their regular holiday business was on a more compact scale, confined to the wealthier sections of society and in considerable contrast to the mass market which was, happily, about to emerge.

The firm of T. Llewelyn Davies continued in business until 1969, when the two brothers sold out to Ellerman Travel, for whom they continued to work, Lloyd taking up the post of managing director in Scotland. He retired in 1980 but stayed on for another three years in an advisory role, finally giving up when he was 75. He had seen it all, served as president of the Scottish Passenger Agents and chairman of ABTA in Scotland. He had come to know and respect Jim Moffat, through the various travel organisations and had enjoyed his company on trips abroad, not least an African safari.

Being an established man of travel, he wouldn't have known, from the other side, that Jim Moffat was treading warily as a newcomer and knew his place, which he accepted with all due humility. When he and Margie went to their very first conference of the Association of British Travel Agents, they were delighted to find that it was to be held on a shake-down cruise for the P. & O. ship *Oriana*, sailing from Southampton to Lisbon and back. As newcomers who were little countenanced even by their fellow-Scots, they knew there would be a pecking order and were therefore not too surprised to be allocated a cabin which was not so much a cabin, more a two-bunk cupboard on the ninth deck. Jim Moffat and Margie look back with wry amusement on that early experience when now, on their various invitations, they find their elevated status has taken them from a dingy cupboard to a suite, all geared to the size of your business overturn.

Jim Moffat did not think for a minute, in those early days, that he would ever be competing with the big names of the trade but soon he was meeting people like Lloyd Davies and hearing of conditions in the days before he ventured into travel. Accompanying him on that safari to Rhodesia, for example, he learned that Lloyd had undertaken the same trip before the Second World War – in a flying-boat which had to land at Venice Harbour and took a week to reach Africa. That was the kind of anecdote Lloyd Davies could summon up in remembering life in his father's company. It may have served mainly a top-level clientèle but that amounted to a large volume of business – and it had all been done from one busy office in Queen Street, Glasgow.

With modern trends and pressures, it is not uncommon for older people to say they are glad to be out of whatever it is that was their business. Lloyd Davies is no exception. "It seems to me there are too many travel agents nowadays," he says. "The danger I see for the existing ones is that the tour operators will eventually sell directly to the public, which is not a very good outlook for the smaller agent."

So he retired to his villa in Newton Mearns, to become more of a holiday-maker than a maker of holidays. That family name which had established such a

Travel Agents bound for Africa, Jim Moffat half way up steps on right, Lloyd Davies bottom right.

reputation in the heart of Glasgow was swallowed up in the Ellerman buy-out (Lloyd Davies wishes now he had inserted a clause about retaining the name) and that, in turn, was sold to Lunn Poly. They moved out of the premises at 21 Queen Street, which became a toy shop and then a florist's.

But fate plays some strange tricks. A.T. MAYS were also in Queen Street but, because of re-development, Scottish Metropolitan Property asked Jim Moffat to move to another address in the same street – at none other than number 21! With the refurbishing of Lewis's in Argyle Street, Jim Moffat saw a future for that end of Queen Street and was doubly happy to locate himself in the former home of a famous name in Scottish travel.

So the old building is back in the travel business, with an A.T. MAYS sign at the front. But round the side, the name of T. Llewelyn Davies has been left in its faded form, still there as a happy symbol of a story which tells of one great name which set high standards in the Scottish travel business and another which has tried to maintain them, while at the same time becoming the largest agency Scotland has ever seen.

CHAPTER EIGHTEEN

Airways and Fairways

AS the only son of Jim and Margie, Jamie Moffat was born in 1950 and has vague memories of his father's last days as a disenchanted bank clerk. He would go down to the bottom of the road to meet him coming home for tea.

The memory sharpens considerably when you talk about the change-over from bank clerk to small-town businessman, for Jamie has a clear recollection – with picture to prove it – of that opening day at the ALL PETS shop which so petrified sister Margaret. The photograph shows the five-year-old Jamie Moffat resplendent in kilt with the python wrapped round his neck! By then he had started school and Margaret used to take him down to the pet shop after school and also to the travel shop across the road. They would play in the back garden of that original hut, overlooking the railway, while their parents were at work.

Jamie went to Ardrossan Academy and then on to Drumley House preparatory school, near Ayr, after his 11-plus examination. At 14 he moved to Strathallan, the prestigious boys' school in Perthshire, which was less of a traumatic experience for Jamie than for most boys since his parents' involvement in business had left him to develop a fair measure of independence and self-reliance.

At Strathallan he immersed himself in cricket and rugby and, to an increasing extent, in golf. He had already picked up the game from his father and had taken lessons at West Kilbride Golf Club, the family having moved to the popular

Ayrshire residential spot. While at Drumley, he had seen boys with golf clubs and felt a natural affinity with the sport, which would come to fruition at a later stage. At Strathallan, one of the masters thought they should build a golf course around the rugby pitches and Jamie became deeply involved in the creation of that six-hole course. At 14, you might not have picked him out for his golfing talents but, by the time he left Strathallan, he was competing in the Scottish Boys' Championship and had reached a handicap of four by the age of 19. During his time at university, however, he suddenly became a first-class player, down to scratch, and went on to become first the Scottish Universities Golf Champion before winning the British title as well. His double blue for both the Universities of Glasgow and Strathclyde may well be a unique honour. Back home, for good measure, he won the Ayrshire Championship too.

The two universities are explained by the fact that Jamie took an honours degree in bio-chemistry at Strathclyde and followed it up with a diploma course in

Jamie Moffat winning Ayrshire Championship 1971.

Jamie with Telly Savalas, and Murdo McLeod of Celtic, at Pro-Am Golf, Renfrew.

management studies at the business school of Glasgow University. Throughout his university career, though, Jamie had not decided what he was going to do for a job. Though there were no pressures from home, he was in the classic situation of the only son being looked upon as a successor to his father. Bio-chemistry had not exactly been the ideal preparation for a business career and that spell at Glasgow University gave him time to consider the matter further.

Looking back, Jamie says: "Any son of a successful father has this question in his mind about going into the family business. Everyone knows there are certain disadvantages. As it happens, my father and I get on well but it can lead to a fairly turbulent existence. Having heard a lot of business talk around the house from the age of five, I wasn't wholly convinced that I even wanted to get involved in that.

137

"University opened up a whole new world for me. I enjoyed it thoroughly and it gave me time to consider options like accountancy, which would have been a great advantage."

In 1974, however, the matter was resolved when Jamie decided to join his father at A.T. MAYS, laying himself open to the inevitable comparisons of father-and-son but now determined to give it a try anyway. His first posting was as a clerk at the Havelock Street branch, off Byres Road, Glasgow, which had been his father's first foray into the city. Predictably, it was slightly awkward being the boss's son but the manager, an old head, took him under his wing, gave him specific jobs to do and pointed him in the right directions.

Jamie spent some time working for the company's Caledonian Tours, which ran Scottish bus tours, and was then sent to A.T. MAYS at Irvine. From there he went to headquarters in Saltcoats to work in the accounts department, with his mother. Caledonian Tours then ran into some problems, young Jamie was sent to resolve them and returned to Saltcoats to be personal assistant to Alan Bromfield, who was then general manager.

A.T. MAYS had consultancy work undertaken by the Air Travel Training Board, which observed that the company was not tackling its marketing properly. So Jamie was let loose as marketing manager, organising the promotions, advertising, window displays for the branches and so on. He then became marketing director and retail director, responsible for the branches. In more recent times he was appointed managing director, which placed him third in rank with A.T. MAYS, coming after his father as chairman and Sam Newlands as chief executive. Meanwhile, in 1978, he had married Louise Duvall, whose father was a dentist in Edinburgh. They settled in West Kilbride, like Jim and Margie, and have two children, Laura and Ben.

The rate of growth at A.T. MAYS is evident from the fact that Jamie Moffat remembers it, when he joined as recently as 1974, as a modest business, geared to the West of Scotland. Within the organisation, however, there was the drive and initiative to make branch expansion a reality, whether it came from cold starts or from takeovers.

With the selling of the company to the Royal Bank, Jamie acknowledges that some might have viewed it as a matter of Jim Moffat disposing of his son's business inheritance, not that he was exactly leaving him penniless in the process! Jamie sees it as the best possible compromise, by which the Moffat family remained to run the business as if it were still their own, with a financial incentive towards

Jamie Moffat, son of the founder.

that end, not that personal pride would have allowed anything other than a loving stewardship of A.T. MAYS.

"I could have no complaints about the Royal Bank deal," said Jamie. "I had my small shareholding in the company which had been converted into something which was of value. The terms of the sale meant my job and my future were secure and we were still in control of the business. From my point of view, if Dad had sold to Hogg Robinson, for example, I would have been under pressure to satisfy new bosses. There is a logic in what has happened and it is working out well. The Royal Bank said they would not try to influence the way the business was run and they have been true to their word. They cause our financial people a few head-aches to satisfy the demands of their accounting processes but that is all. The funds are available and we could not have continued our rate of expansion from our own resources."

While Jamie Moffat feels it is hard to imagine A.T. MAYS without his father, he is nevertheless ready to take whatever leading position befalls him. He concedes he would like to be chairman one day but knows there may be others before him, perhaps a Royal Bank appointee. Meanwhile he develops his strengths, which lie now in a sound knowledge of the travel business. He has certainly been through enough of it to have gathered a great deal of experience and know-how, not to mention a collection of anecdotes. Even during his university days he was helping out in extraordinary events such as that mass exodus of Rangers' supporters to Barcelona in 1972. In his early days of marketing, he organised film shows for the customers and there are vivid memories of the things that can go wrong with a projector. He recalls standing at the back of the hall in East Kilbride one night and suddenly realising that the reel of film had shot off the machine and was rolling among the patrons. There was the embarrassing night at Renfrew when only four people turned up. Matters could only improve from that, however, and Jamie went on to organise the Holiday Exhibitions at the Magnum in Irvine, extending to Prestwick Airport and the Scottish Exhibition and Conference Centre in Glasgow, where crowds of 5,000 to 6,000 turn up every year.

Nowadays he explains the routine at the Nineyards Street headquarters of A.T. MAYS as a matter of Sam Newlands running the business side, Jamie himself running the travel side – and his father running them both! In fact, the chairman's office in that former bank building is still the hub of activity. The first two hours of any day are spent with the main executives never far away from the chairman's desk. Jamie can be found, in the morning, going through the mail with his father,

140

chatting about what needs to be done. Sam Newlands, Alan Bromfield and Lindsay Grattan will all be there as well. Then Jamie will be off on his visits to various branches to find out what is happening.

Acknowledging that the role of following a successful father is not an easy one, for all its apparent advantages, he looks on the position philosophically: "I realise I could not have been at Drumley and Strathallan if it had not been for my father and the business he built up. I have never had to ask for anything, never wanted for anything. At the same time, my father has never thrown money in my direction and has tried to be sensible about these things. But of course I have had the advantage of always living in a nice house, enjoying good holidays and having no financial worries at university for example.

"Within a year of graduating, I was involved in chats about corporate strategy and I have the advantage, above all, of being in a job which I thoroughly enjoy, involved at the highest level from the earliest stage. So I have been extremely lucky.

"Problems can arise when, as father and son, you forget in which environment you are working. One of you may be thinking 'family' and one is thinking 'business'. We have had the odd barney but mostly from the fact that he was talking to me in my role as retail director – and I thought he was talking to me as my Dad!

"But I have no great conscious feeling that people are comparing me to my father. That doesn't trouble me. I know that I am not my father. I know his strengths compared to my own and I couldn't be the same man as he is. But I am my own man and, in the end, that is what counts."

CHAPTER NINETEEN

Jim Joins an Airline

AS a man whose success has been born of a strange mixture of naivety and shrewdness, Jim Moffat retains the looks of someone who might easily have become lost in the by-ways of life, remaining in the obscurity of a bank clerk's cubby-hole or breeding budgies in his aviary while the world passed him by. Barbara Kelly and her panel in *What's My Line?* would probably have guessed him to be a small-time Ayrshire farmer with a few dairy cows and a touch of eccentricity in his nature.

A natural shyness of manner seems to fit him uncertainly for the maelstrom of modern business yet the consistency of his success could too easily be put down to some incredibly fortuitous chain of events, in which he just happened to bounce from one right decision to another. Such things seldom happen in the real world. Beneath the slightly fey exterior of Jim Moffat there lies a brain that works exceedingly well, linked to an instinct for wise decisions which is indispensible to every man or woman who hopes to survive for a lifetime in the hurly-burly of business.

While he has surrendered the dream of seeing his business baby retain its sturdy independence for all of his own lifetime, he takes a philosophical view of it all, finding some amusement in the fact that board meetings under the aegis of the Royal Bank are efficiently matter-of-fact affairs, with strict note-taking and serious attitudes, whereas they used to be conducted with an air of informality which came close to the pleasantries of a chat-show.

As he approached his 70th birthday in 1989, he was not only looking back over a fascinating career but casting an eye ahead to the future of the travel industry. What did he see in the crystal ball?

"I think the graph of holiday business, which has been constantly on the up-swing in these post-war years, will continue to rise, though perhaps not so rapidly. But, as long as people like Boeing keep on turning out bigger aircraft, the airlines and tour operators will want to fill seats.

"And as long as A.T. MAYS remains in the top bracket of agencies, we shall hold our fair percentage of the business. Much of this hinges on the country's economy and on people's disposable income. The public have become accustomed to their fridges, freezers, microwaves and stereos and into that cat-egory of expectation comes the family holiday.

"Of course business can fluctuate but people are now looking further and further afield. Long-distance experts, like Speedbird and Kuoni, now find it difficult to keep up with the demand for information about the Far East. The £1,000 holiday may still be a big item in Scotland but, in the stockbroker belt and those well-heeled corners of England we keep hearing about, such a price is commonplace. They may still go to their former Mediterranean resorts but they are now just as keen to see Bangkok, Bali, Barbados or the far distance of Australia.

"Through all the added adventure, there are still big bookings in what is known in the trade as VFR – Visit Friends and Relations – which is now such a simple undertaking compared to those earlier days when relatives departed for Canada and Australia believing they may never see their families again. Some never did. But now all that is changed."

Without a trace of the pretentious, Jim Moffat can say in all sincerity that he regards his business as one in which, progress and profit apart, he has genuinely felt that he was doing people some good, helping them not only to broaden their horizons but to improve their health as well. Without being too specific, he hints that there are areas of selling to the public where his conscience would not have rested too easily. That just happens to be the kind of man he is.

And that sense of personal care about the customer has filtered across to the public at large, as you discover by wandering into an A.T. MAYS office and talking to people at random. You are liable to run into someone like Pat McLaughlin from West Kilbride, a retired carpenter who used to work locally with

ICI. Pat and his wife knew little about travel until 1967, when their daughter Marlene treated them to two weeks in Majorca as a silver wedding present. That was just the start of their adventures, as they came more and more to rely on the staff at A.T. MAYS to book their holidays. Having once found their way to the sun, they kept going every year to one of the Mediterranean resorts, whether in Majorca, Ibiza or mainland Spain.

When daughter Marlene got married and emigrated to Vancouver, the horizons were extended even further. Mrs McLaughlin has been to visit her daughter no fewer than 12 times and Pat has been there nine times. Pat's retirement years have coincided largely with the boom years of investment, from 1980, and the return on his savings has largely financed his safaris. That was just as well, for his son, John, followed his sister's example and set out for foreign parts too, this time to Perth, Western Australia. The parents were not to be outdone on that one either. Three times they have been out to see John on visits which have included a round-the-world tour and taken in Hawaii, Disneyland – and the football World Cup in Mexico!

"We wouldn't have been travelling with A.T. MAYS all these years if there had not been something special in their service," is Pat's way of paying tribute to the company. "There is a personal touch about it and, having come to know Jim Moffat, I also know that he is such a nice man who sets the standards."

Willie Gall, the well-known newspaper cartoonist, is another who volunteers good opinions about the founder of A.T. MAYS: "In 1937, I was working as a traveller for McVittie and Price and stayed in digs in Saltcoats, along with a chap who worked in the local branch of the National Bank. That was how I came to know a colleague of his, the young bank clerk whose name was Jim Moffat. We went around together as a group, playing golf and so on. He was a quiet young man but I could see he wasn't happy with his lot in the bank. Obviously, he must have had a flair for business and his success is astonishing.

"I don't suppose I have seen him since just after the war but, when I published my recent book of cartoons, I had a delightful letter from Jim, saying how much it had brightened his festive season. He hadn't forgotten after all those years – and it was fairly typical of the young lad I remembered."

The personal touch which Jim Moffat instilled in the dealings of A.T. MAYS does not become any easier to maintain in a world where computerisation has come to dominate. A.T. MAYS is now linked into a network, with mysterious machines which can issue tickets and invoices and feed it all back to headquarters for information and storage.

But the Moffats allow nothing to deflect attention from the vast number of people who have helped to make their business what it has become. "At one time," says Margie, "I thought we should list ourselves as a marriage bureau, such was the number of office romances, starting with Lindsay Grattan, now our personnel director, who married Mary McConnell."

Margie points to the advance in aviation as the biggest change in her experience, recalling the days when the only means of going abroad was through London, often by bus or overnight railway journey. "At that time, the holiday traffic was all in the summer months and, from October to December, we relied on business travel and emigration to keep us occupied. Then more package tour firms moved on to air travel and a few daring spirits started flying from Glasgow. To keep their aircraft flying, they brought in cheap weekend winter tours to Majorca, which gave more and more people a taste of the sun. We were delighted to be kept busy all year round.

"The other side of the coin was the departure of regular sailings from Ardrossan to Ireland and the Isle of Man. We used to charter those ships for day tours on Sundays and for special occasions, like the Orange Walk. It was quite a spectacle to see them sailing off with their bands and banners, some adventurous spirits climbing masts and sometimes leaping from the quay just as the ship was leaving."

So much for the memories. But the sell-out to the Royal Bank of Scotland and the prospect of stepping down as chairman in 1992 was not to signal the departure of Jim Moffat from business life. Having retained a connection with several business ventures, he made one more commitment during the months leading to his 70th birthday. With money to invest after the Royal Bank deal, he showed faith in Scottish enterprise by taking a five per cent financial stake in Scottish European Airways, a fledgling airline which sought to establish direct links between Scotland and the continent. Many a small airline had tried and failed but the chairman of the new company, Roger Barnard, had undertaken some serious research and gathered around him an experienced team of people, like David Short, as managing director, Gordon Mason as marketing director, Robin Gibbs in commercial planning, Michael Hughes in engineering and Captain Murdo MacDonald in charge of air operations.

They bought over the prop-jet aeroplanes formerly operated by the unfortunate Chieftain Airways and took to the air in November 1988, with direct daily services to Brussels and Frankfurt, also gaining what is known as "the fifth freedom" to uplift passengers flying between these two points, a privilege not usually enjoyed by foreign airlines. With a total staff of 40 and a return fare to Frankfurt for as little as £125, the company made an immediate appeal to many businessmen seeking a day's visit to the continent. Needless to say, it was proving invaluable to Scotland's Euro MPs, like Winnie Ewing and Hugh McMann, and offering a service generally regarded as even better than that of the business class at the former British Caledonian, where Gordon Mason had worked for many years.

Jim Moffat's experience of the business and life-long interest in aeroplanes and what they can provide was clearly a boost to the new company, which was anxious to succeed where others may have failed.

CHAPTER TWENTY

Back Home with the Budgies

HOME today for Jim and Margie Moffat is in a secluded villa called Sarala, in West Kilbride, with its French windows opening out to a terraced garden, giving a magnificent view of the Firth of Clyde and looking directly across to the Isle of Arran.

From the bungalow in Ardrossan which Jim had inherited from his parents, they had come to West Kilbride one day to help find a house for an Aer Lingus manager. Jim Moffat took an instant liking to the village and decided he wanted to move there himself. He found a semi-detached house which tided them over till they landed the house he and Margie really wanted. The elderly lady who owned Sarala had lived in India in earlier life and was intrigued to find a prospective buyer who had served there during the war. She took an instant liking to Jim Moffat and wanted him to be the new owner of her house, so much so that she informed the estate agent she did not want anyone else looking it over! If Mr Moffat would raise his offer by £500, it was his. So for £9,500, still a sizeable sum in 1963, the Moffats moved into Sarala, which is a Hindustani word meaning The Beautiful Place, and that is exactly what it is.

There, Jim and Margie live a fairly simple life, espousing the theory of many rich people that you can wear only one suit and eat so much in a day. There are people on more modest incomes who enjoy as many extras as the Moffats, give

Jim Moffat at home – with his magnificent view across the Clyde to Arran.

or take perhaps the added comfort of the Daimler Sovereign, the ability to take off on that Caribbean cruise at will – and that magnificent view across to Arran.

Predictably, they have travelled to most of the attractive corners of the globe (though Margie paid her visit to Oban only recently!) and are in total agreement about the country they would place at the very top of their list. Saddened by its internal troubles, the Moffats are nevertheless in no doubt that South Africa is the most beautiful country in the world and have particular memories of sailing there on the cruise ship, *Windsor Castle*.

By the early Seventies, A.T. MAYS had grown in size to the point where the Moffats were welcomed into British Airways Top Twenty Club, an exclusive group of travel agents who are wooed and fêted by the big airline all the way from luxury cruises to a flight on Concorde to Mexico City, with all the trimmings of first-class attention. By then they had indeed come a long way from that cupboard on the *Oriana*.

150

Jim Moffat – happy with his budgies but always a phone at hand.

Back home, at the bottom of his garden in West Kilbride, Jim Moffat retreats to his life-long pleasure of breeding budgies, that pastime to which he was introduced by his father in early life. "It is a hobby which is difficult to describe to people," he says. "The budgie is really the poor man's racehorse. You are breeding it for show and sometimes for sale. Ten years ago I was quite a prominent breeder but now I am less so. I still keep about 300 birds and breed for shape, style and colour. The poorer ones tend to go to the pet shops for sale. I suppose I have sold a budgie for £100 but they can go much higher. There was a recent sale of a budgie to a Japanese gentleman for £2,500."

With all the trappings of their business success, Jim and Margie Moffat still go to work every day, at the A.T. MAYS headquarters in Nineyards Street. They drive home for lunch together and, as they pass along the seafront at Saltcoats on a summer day, they find it an abiding pleasure to see perhaps 40 or 50 girls in the distinctive RAF blue blouse, with red scarf, which marks them out as employees of A.T. MAYS.

Jim and Margie Moffat, the founding team, with Jim's portrait in background.

"I must confess," says Jim, "that I feel jolly proud to think that, if we have done nothing else in life, we have put these girls into uniforms and given them worthwhile careers. It is really satisfying to know that we have created a structure of career for so many people, particularly in North Ayrshire, where there has never been a surfeit of jobs."

Thus Jim and Margie Moffat find the overriding satisfaction of their lives, a union which began in the turbulence of the Second World War, with little hint of what lay ahead. Even the move from disgruntled bank clerk to business novice in a little wooden hut would scarcely have inspired a prediction of great things to come.

But the progress of Jim Moffat developed into an adventure tale which pays yet another tribute to that traditional ability of the Scots to make their mark. It is also a clear case of encouragement to succeeding generations, making it plain that the road to prosperity is never closed to those with the right amount of drive and determination – and that glimmer of vision which keeps us going on this long and winding path.

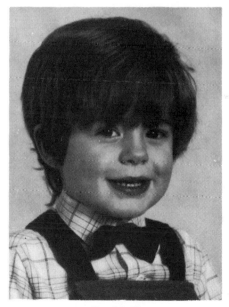

Ben Moffat.

153

Laura Moffat.

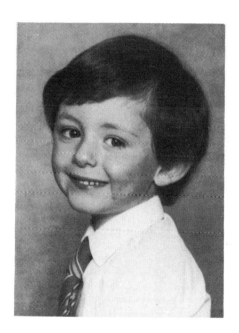

James Borges.